Green-Wood Illustrated: In Highly Finished Line Engraving, From Drawings Taken On The Spot

James Smillie

In the interest of creating a more extensive selection of rare historical book reprints, we have chosen to reproduce this title even though it may possibly have occasional imperfections such as missing and blurred pages, missing text, poor pictures, markings, dark backgrounds and other reproduction issues beyond our control. Because this work is culturally important, we have made it available as a part of our commitment to protecting, preserving and promoting the world's literature. Thank you for your understanding.

GREEN-WOOD

ILLUSTRATED.

IN

Highly Finished Line Engraving,

FROM DRAWINGS TAKEN ON THE SPOT,

BY JAMES SMILLIE.

WITH

DESCRIPTIVE NOTICES,

BY NEHEMIAH CLEAVELAND.

NEW YORK:

PUBLISHED BY R. MARTIN, 170 BROADWAY.

1847.

Entered according to Act of Congress, in the year 1847,
By ROBERT MARTIN,
In the Clerk's Office of the District Court of the United States for the Southern District of New York.

LIST OF ENGRAVINGS.

MAP,		*(to face vignette.)*	
VIEW OF THE ENTRANCE,			PAGE 8
" "	KEEPER'S LODGE,		10
" "	POET'S MOUND,		13
" "	OCEAN HILL,		15
" "	INDIAN MOUND,		19
" "	BAY-SIDE AVENUE,		26
" "	BAY-GROVE HILL,		26
VIEW FROM THE GROUND INTENDED FOR THE CLINTON MONUMENT,			40
VIEW OF THE TOUR FROM OAKEN BLUFF,			40
" "	" FERN HILL,		41
" "	LAWN-GIRT HILL,		61
" "	TOUR FROM OCEAN HILL,		62
" "	SYLVAN CLIFF,		63
" "	GROUNDS OF THE CHURCH OF OUR SAVIOUR, (Vista Hill,)		65
" "	GRECIAN OBELISK, (Ocean Hill,)		73
" "	BATTLE HILL,		79
" "	PILOT'S MONUMENT,		92
" "	GERMAN LOTS, AND THE ODD-FELLOWS' GROUNDS,		94

GREEN-WOOD.

> " The hills,
> Rock-ribbed and ancient as the sun;—the vales,
> Stretching in pensive quietness between ;—
> The venerable woods"—
>   " and pour'd round all,
> Old ocean's gray and melancholy waste—
> Are but the solemn decorations all,
> Of the great tomb of man."
>   BRYANT.

IT is fifteen years since Mount Auburn, near Boston, was set apart as a place of sepulture. It was the first attempt in this country, to meet a want which had long been felt. Happily conceived, and well executed, it soon led the way to similar enterprises in other cities; and now, there is scarcely a large town which has not, in its neighborhood, a rural cemetery. To regard this great movement as merely imitative, or fashionable, would be doing it injustice. The impropriety of making interments beneath and around churches, and in the festering burial-grounds of cities, was generally acknowledged. Injurious to health, offensive to the senses, repulsive to the taste of a refined age, the practice had become a confessed nuisance, which all desired, but none knew how to abate. Long usage, invested capital, the affections themselves, which make us wish to be laid by the side of those we have loved,—all combined to perpetuate the evil.

The idea of a rural cemetery, sufficiently remote to be beyond the range of city improvements, yet so near as to be of convenient access, seemed to reach, at once, all the necessities of the case. Large enough for the wants of many generations, it furnishes, in its guarded enclosure, full security against those violations of the grave, by which the zeal of science or of gain has so often shocked public sentiment, and deeply injured the feelings of survivors. The vault, so unpleasant to many, might indeed be found here, but it would no longer be the inevitable resting-place of the departed. Hither wounded Affection could resort, attracting no notice, and dreading no intrusion. Here Sorrow could bring its graceful offerings, and Taste and Art join with Nature herself, in adorning the last home of the loved and lost. To its silent solitudes the thoughtful would come to meditate;—here the man of business and care would often reassure his hesitating virtue;—and here, amid the thousand witnesses of mortality, and in all the soothing influences of the scene, the gay and reckless would read lessons of wisdom and piety.

To the importance of this reform, New York, though somewhat slow to move, could not but at length awake. If anywhere the evils alluded to were obvious and vast; if in any city better accommodations were imperatively demanded, that city was, emphatically, this great and growing metropolis. Again and again, in the progress of improvement, the fields of the dead had been broken up, to be covered with buildings, or converted into open squares. The tables of death showed that, already, nearly ten thousand human bodies must be annually interred: while calculation made it all but certain that, in half a century more, the aggregate would be told in millions.

The island of New York presenting no secure, or at least no very

INTRODUCTION.

eligible spot for a cemetery, attention was turned to a large, unoccupied tract in Brooklyn, lying near Gowanus Bay. As if providentially designed and reserved for the very use to which it has been put, it would be difficult to name a particular in which these grounds could have been better adapted to that use. Within sight of the thronged mart, and not three miles from its busiest haunts, GREEN-WOOD enjoys, nevertheless, perfect seclusion. It is of ample extent, and there is hardly a square rod of it which may not be used for burial. Its numerous avenues and paths furnish a long and delightful drive, presenting continually, scenes of varied beauty. Now you pass over verdant and sunny lawns,—now through park-like groves,—and now by the side of a tangled, unpruned forest. At one moment, you are in the dell, with its still waters, its overhanging shade, and its sweet repose. At the next, you look out from the hill-top, on the imperial city, with its queenly daughter—on the bay, so beautiful and life-like—down into the quiet, rural hamlet—or beyond it, on the distant ocean.

GREEN-WOOD CEMETERY was incorporated in 1838, but from various causes, did not commence successful operations till four years later. Its charter, with some amendments since made, embraces every desirable provision for the security, permanence, and proper government of the institution.

It authorizes and directs the land acquired by the corporation, to be disposed of and used exclusively for the burial of the dead.

It exempts such lands forever from assessment, and from all public taxes; and also from all liability to be sold on execution, or for the payment of debts by assignment under any insolvent law.

It requires that, when the payment of the purchase-money of the land shall have been made, "the proceeds of ALL future sales shall be applied to the preservation, improvement, and embellishment of the said Cemetery, and to the incidental expenses thereof, and to NO OTHER PURPOSE WHATEVER."

It authorizes the corporation to hold, upon trust, any donation or bequest of property, and to apply the same, or the income thereof, for the improvement or embellishment of the Cemetery, or for the erection, repair, preservation, or renewal of any tomb, monument, or fence, or for the planting and cultivation of trees, shrubs, flowers, or plants, in or around any cemetery lot, or for improving the said premises in any other form or manner, consistent with the design of the charter, and conformably to the terms of such grant or bequest.

Every proprietor of a lot or parcel of ground containing not less than three hundred square feet, may vote at any election for Trustees of the Corporation; and the Trustees, fifteen in number, must in all cases be chosen from among the proprietors of the lots.

Thus it appears that proprietors of lots acquire not merely the privilege of burial, but the fee-simple of the ground which they purchase;—that, being the sole owners of the Cemetery, they, by their vote in the election of Trustees, control, directly, the government of the institution;—that no pecuniary, or other conflicting interest can exist, to counteract the general wishes of the lot-owners;—and that, as the lots are not subject to public charge, nor held liable for debts, nor subject to assessment by the institution, they can never be forcibly taken from the purchasers.

The grounds comprise about one hundred and eighty-five acres. Arrangements for extending these limits are in progress, which will give, when completed, an area of two hundred and fifty acres. Although now much larger than any other of our cemeteries, it will

INTRODUCTION.

scarcely, even in its contemplated increase, be proportioned to the wants of the great and fast-augmenting population, which it is designed to accommodate. That population is already nearly a half-million; and if the past be prophetic of the future, it will take years only, or tens of years, to make New York, in point of magnitude, what centuries and tens of centuries have made Paris and London. It is then but a wise forecast, thus liberally to provide for the sure and fast-coming future. The ground will all be wanted—it will be all used. Those already exist, who will behold it when it shall have become a vast city of the Dead, outnumbering that of the living by its side.

Only four years have elapsed since GREEN-WOOD was publicly opened for interments. Within that time, about fourteen hundred lots have been sold. The avenues, which wind gracefully over every part of its undulating surface, for an extent of more than ten miles, have been put into perfect order. With a judicious regard to both utility and effect, the natural conformation of the ground has, in many instances, been somewhat varied and improved. The trees, a prominent feature of the place, have generally been preserved, though here and there removed, to open vistas through the copse, and make the grounds more available or more picturesque. Much work has been done in removing every unsightly object and obstruction, and in enriching and beautifying the yet unoccupied space. Of the purchased lots, a large proportion are neatly and substantially enclosed by iron paling; while monuments and sepulchral structures, already numerous, and many of them new and beautiful in design, consecrate and embellish the ground.

In one respect GREEN-WOOD differs, it is believed, from every similar institution;—a peculiarity which it owes, partly, to its ample accommodations and natural facilities, and still more, to judicious regulations adopted at the outset. Reference is made to the appropriation of large lots for the use of families and societies. Taking advantage of the natural inequalities, the summits and sides of the knolls have been enclosed in circles or ellipses, as their shape and position required. By the greater size, as well as by the form of these lots, and the introduction, in some cases, of other figures, much has been done to avoid the rigid sameness, which would result from a division of the whole surface into equal parallelograms. By giving wider spaces between the lots, it tends to prevent crowding and confusion, when funerals are numerously attended; and though some space is lost to purposes of interment, it is secured for beauty and for a higher utility.

But it is the provision which it makes for associated families, and for religious and other communities, which gives to this arrangement its chief value. Not only may the single family enjoy the solace of feeling that they have secured for themselves one guarded and hallowed spot, but its kindred and affiliated branches can make common cause, and the ties of friendship and consanguinity shall become stronger in life, when they shall not seem wholly severed at the grave.

Again, those whose bond of union has been community of sentiment,—who have been associated in labors of self-improvement and of benevolence,—who have listened so often in the same sanctuary, to those lessons of faith and hope, which alone can take from death its sting, and from the grave its victory,—may here lie down, the rich and the poor together, as was the wont of old, in their own church-yard.

Several religious societies have secured grounds in the Cemetery. One church has already enclosed a large and handsome mound, and

INTRODUCTION.

consecrated it to its use with appropriate rites. Around its circumference are the lots of individual members, while an inner circle is reserved for the Pastor and for those of humbler means. It was a happy and a Christian thought, to provide for their poorer brethren, when the toils of life shall be over, an unexpensive resting-place, as respectable and beautiful as their own. The example is well worthy of imitation.

THE ENTRANCE.

> "Enter this wild-wood,
> And view the haunts of Nature. The calm shade
> Shall bring a kindred calm, and the sweet breeze
> That makes the green leaves dance, shall waft a balm
> To thy sick heart."

GREEN-WOOD occupies a portion of the high ground which separates Gowanus Bay from the plains of Flatbush. The most agreeable, though not the shortest route, is the ancient road running from Brooklyn along the western shore of Long Island, to Fort Hamilton. At the distance of two and a half miles from the South Ferry, a short, straight avenue leads from the main street of Gowanus to the gate.

The entrance is perfectly simple. On the left of the gate is a rustic lodge, for the temporary accommodation of visiters. On the right, and in the same style, is a small tower, with a bell to summon the Porter. These unambitious structures will be found in good keeping with each other, and with the position they occupy. They possess beauty of form, and of fitness likewise. Perhaps some, accustomed to more imposing entrances, may feel disappointed by the modest humility of this. But may not the taste at least be questioned, which makes the passage-way from one open space to another, through some lofty arch, or massive building? Can such a structure look well, with no support, on either side of it, but an ordinary fence? Must it not always lack

the beauty of adaptation to an end—the essential beauty of usefulness?
And if it be, as most frequently, of Grecian or Egyptian model, is it not
incongruous with the spirit and associations of a Christian cemetery?
Of the simple entrance temporarily made for these grounds, we may at
least say, that here Art raises no false expectation, nor does it offend
by unnatural contrasts. But, enter. If the artificial portal be deficient
in dignity, not so will you find that of Nature. You are now in a ves-
tibule of her own making. Its floor is a delicious greensward; its walls
are the steep hill-side; lofty trees, with their leafy capitals, form its
colonnade; and its ceiling is the azure vault. Here, if alive to gentle
influences, you will pause a moment. You will shake from your feet
the city's dust, and leave behind you its care and follies. You are
within the precinct of a great, primeval temple, now forever set apart
to pious uses. You have come,

> "Not to the domes where crumbling arch and column
>   Attest the feebleness of mortal hand;
> But to that fane most catholic and solemn,
>   Which God hath planned!"

Explore its aisles and courts,—survey its beauties,—breathe its fresh
air,—enjoy its quiet,—drink in its music,—and lay to heart its lessons
of mortality, as well as its higher teachings of faith and love.

THE KEEPER'S LODGE.

> "A voice from 'the Green-Wood!'—a voice! and it said,
> 'Ye have chosen me out as a home for your dead;
> From the bustle of life ye have render'd me free;
> My earth ye have hallow'd: henceforth I shall be
> A garden of graves, where your loved ones shall rest!'"

On the left of the avenue, and just beyond the entrance, stands the Keeper's Lodge. It is a cottage in the rustic, pointed style, with four gables. The sides are of plank uprights, battened with cedar poles, rough from the forest. Its whole exterior is unsmoothed and unpainted,—yet it is symmetrical and picturesque. Embowered in the grove, and already looking old enough to be coeval with the trees that shade it, its entire aspect is in harmony with the place and its associations. In such a home, we sometimes imagine, might have been found, long ago, near the church-yard of some quiet hamlet in our fatherland, one of those immortal sextons, whose occupation and quaint humor genius has loved to depict.

Hard by, a tower of the same primitive order supports a bell, which is rung whenever a funeral train enters the grounds. This is a custom hallowed by its own appropriateness, as well as by long and general observance. In cities, the tolling of bells for the dead has, as a matter of necessity, been long discontinued. In country villages, however, the usage still prevails. The deep tones of the bell in Green-Wood, penetrating its dells, and echoing from its hills, are the only sounds that

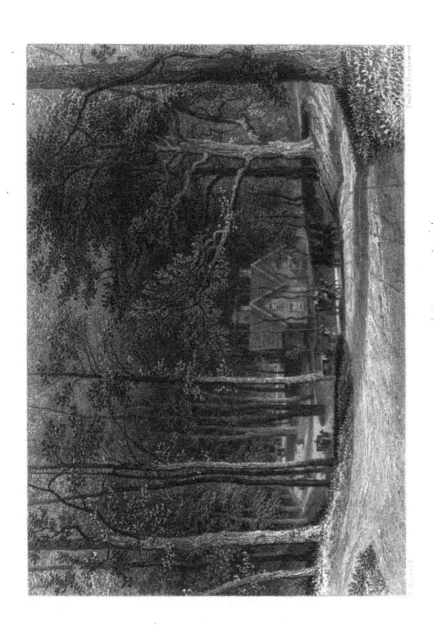

THE KEEPER'S LODGE. 11

reach the mourner's ear, as he follows some dear object to the tomb. Often, we know, at such times, this unexpected but still familiar sound has touched the springs of memory and feeling, carrying back the mind to the homely scenes, but bright hours of childhood,—to the far-off, native vale,—to that knell from the village steeple, which once called the reminiscent to weep over some sweet flower, cut down in its morning beauty,—and to that humble grave-yard, where, bedewed with tears of veneration and love, a father and mother now sleep, side by side.

A mournful office is thine, old bell,
To ring forth naught but the last sad knell
Of the coffin'd worm, as he passeth by,—
And thou seemest to say, Ye all must die!

No joyful peal dost thou ever ring;
But ever and aye, as hither they bring
The dead to sleep 'neath the " Green-Wood" tree,
Thy voice is heard, pealing mournfully.

No glad occasion dost thou proclaim—
Thy mournful tone is ever the same;—
The slow, measured peal, that tells of wo
Such as those who feel it may only know.

Had thy tongue the power of speech, old bell,
Methinks strange stories 'twould often tell;
How some are brought hither with tear and moan,
While others pass by, unmourn'd, alone;—

How strangers are hither brought to sleep,
Whose home, perchance, was beyond the deep,—
Who, seeking our shore, came but to die,
And here in this hallow'd spot to lie;—

How a wife hath follow'd a husband's bier,—
How a husband hath follow'd a wife most dear,—
How brother and sister have come, in turn,
To shed a tear o'er a parent's urn;—

How the victim of sorrow's ceaseless smart
Hath given up life with a willing heart,
And thought of this spot with a smiling face,
Glad at last to find him a resting-place.

I wonder if thou dost ring, old bell,
For the rich man a louder, longer knell,
Than thou dost for the poor who enter here,
On the humble and unpretending bier?

And dost thou ring forth a peal less sad
For the pure and good, than for the bad?
Or dost thou toll the same knell for all—
The rich and the poor, the great and small?

Oh, a mournful office is thine, old bell!
To ring forth naught but the last sad knell
Of the coffin'd worm as he passeth by,
And thou seemest to say, Prepare to die!

ARTHUR MORRELL.

POET'S MOUND.

"From every tree and every bush
There seems to breathe a soothing hush;
While every transient sound but shows
How deep and still is the repose."

SYLVAN WATER is a permanent and deep pond of about four acres.
The visiter, as he passes along the elevated summit of its northern
border, catches, through the foliage, occasional glimpses of its bright
surface. A winding descent soon brings him to its margin, and to a
scene of beauty and stillness where he will love to linger. Except on
the western side, the grounds about it are precipitous and high, and all
round they are closely wooded. The trees and shrubs form, indeed, a
perfect wall of verdure to this secluded little lake, while

"The soft wave, as wrapt in slumber, lies
Beneath the forest-shade."

He who stands upon its verge sees only water, woods, and sky. He
hears naught but the notes, plaintive or lively, of scores of birds, which
haunt this dell, and at times fill it with their music. To the weary and
worn citizen, it may well seem the very ideal of solitude—a charming
picture of repose. Ever since he entered these green-wood shades, he
has been sensibly getting farther and farther away from strife, and

business, and care; at every step he has become more and more imbued with the gentle spirit of the place. But here he finds the illusion and the charm complete. A short half-hour ago, he was in the midst of a discordant Babel; he was one of the hurrying, jostling crowd; he was encompassed by the whirl and fever of artificial life. Now he stands alone, in Nature's inner court—in her silent, solemn sanctuary. Her holiest influences are all around him, and his heart whispers, It is good to be here!

The monument represented in the plate occupies a small knoll on the northern edge of Sylvan Water, and is a tribute paid by friendship to the memory of a child of misfortune. "The poor inhabitant below" was the possessor of talents which, had his mind and affections been better disciplined, might have won for him distinction. But his efforts were desultory and unequal. He became an unhappy wanderer,—his own and others' dupe,—till at length reason tottered, and life sunk under the weight of disappointment.

> "Unskilful he to note the card
> Of prudent lore,
> Till billows raged, and gales blew hard,
> And whelmed him o'er."

The monument is of white marble—a square block, supporting a truncated pyramid. On the northern face of the die is a profile likeness of the poet, in high relief.

McDonald Clarke was born June 18, 1798, and died March 5, 1842.

OCEAN HILL.

"In depth, in height, in circuit, how serene
The spectacle, how pure! Of Nature's works
In earth, and air, and earth-embracing sea,
A revelation beautiful it seems."

THIS is one of the most elevated spots in the Cemetery. It occupies the north-eastern corner of the grounds. Its western and southern sides are steep. Towards the east it declines gently to the plain. The principal avenue, called the Tour, conducts you to its summit, and you find yourself near the northern extremity of a beautiful and commanding ridge. On the north and the south, the prospect is bounded by copse-wood. Through the trees on the western side, may be caught occasional glimpses of the pleasant lawn which you have just crossed. Toward the east the view is unobstructed and wide. From the base of the hill stretch far away the plains of Flatbush and New Utrecht. Below, a short mile distant, lies the little village of Flatbush,—an image of quiet life,—with its white dwellings and simple spire; the Pavilion at Rockaway, some ten miles off, is clearly seen; while the sea itself, with here and there a sail, terminates the view.

The beauties of the eminence seem to be appreciated. Most of the lots on its summit have been already taken and improved. The objects delineated in the plate are those which present themselves to

16   GREEN-WOOD ILLUSTRATED.

one who, having kept along the Tour from the west, has just gained the summit of the hill. The monuments and the cottage at once arrest the eye, and the agreeable impression which they make is due, perhaps, not less to their harmonious grouping, than to their individual beauty. Of the three principal monuments here given, the material is the same, and the style is so far similar, as to require that they should be classed in one family. Yet are they specifically distinct—each having its peculiar merit, and forming a study by itself. The two which are seen in the foreground, were among the earliest of the erections in Green-Wood. The novelty of the designs—their graceful outline—and the high finish of the work, united with a height and magnitude which give dignity and effect—have drawn to them much attention. They set, in this respect, a good example, and they have unquestionably had an influence on the taste and style of many subsequent improvements. They showed that there are beautiful and fitting forms for sepulchral memorials, besides the obelisk, or even the more graceful and classic pillar and sarcophagus. They evinced that a pleasing variety in details is consistent with the same scope of general design, and that in art, as elsewhere, genius is not confined to one idea, nor prone to make fac-similes of its own works. The fault of servile imitation in such matters has been far too common, and a tame monotony is its inevitable effect.

The material employed is the compact, red sandstone from New Jersey, first brought into use in the erection of Trinity Church. The toughness of this stone, and the closeness of its grain, make it, in the plastic hand of the carver, almost if not quite equal to the best marble. No other stone furnished by our quarries, and of equal or even similar facility under the tool, can resist, it is believed, so well, the defacing and destructive effects of our humid and frosty atmosphere, and its ever-changing temperature. If in its youth the freestone structure be less brilliant and attractive than that of marble, it certainly bears its age better. Its surface is less liable to accretions and stains; and those which it does incur, instead of appearing like streaks and patches of dirt, sullying the lustre of that which should be clean and bright, are but time-honored hues and shades, making it more beautiful. These two lots occupy a somewhat salient angle formed by the road, and are, in form, spherical triangles. The coping, which supports a low, neat paling, and the posts at the corners, are of the same stone with the principal structures. The form and finish of these minor parts, and even the grading and shaping of the ground, show that minute attention to particulars which is so essential to harmony and fulness of effect.

The monument on the left is a tripod in the Roman style, supported on the corners by richly carved, antique trusses, and resting on a boldly moulded base course. The die has, on each of its faces, a tablet with circular head. The mouldings of its cornice are simple but effective, and it is surmounted by a well-proportioned urn. Its height is about fourteen feet.

On one of the tablets is recorded the death of a young mother, and that of an only and infant child, which occurred not long before her own. To this simple statement are appended these words from II. Kings, iv. 26 :—"Is it well with thee? Is it well with the child? And she answered, It is well."

The right-hand monument rests upon a square base, with prominent mouldings. The die diminishes upward by a gentle curve; its angles are enriched by a graceful, scolloped leaf, and its cornice is encircled by carved mouldings. Above this, the form changes from square to circular, and a fine urn completes the design.

On the northern side, standing out in strong relief, is a female bust. This face, beautifully executed by Mancini, shows admirably the capacities of the stone for expressive sculpture; and though not intended as a likeness, it calls strongly up the image of that young wife, who, taken from life in the midst of youth, and health, and hope, now rests beneath.

INDIAN MOUND.

—— "thou who o'er thy friend's low bier,
Sheddest the bitter drops like rain,
   Hope that a brighter, happier sphere,
Will give her to thy arms again."

THE grave of Do-HUM-ME is under the lofty trees that shade the northern border of Sylvan Lake. The earth around it, hard-trodden by a thousand feet, bears constant testimony to the sympathy which a tale and fate like hers, never fail to awaken. The impression which her extraordinary grace and beauty made on those who saw her here, is still retained by many, and justifies the glowing picture which is given in the following sketch. The description may be relied on, for it is furnished by one who knew her in her happiness, and who deserted her not when she was sick and dying. Through the same kind instrumentality, a neat marble monument was placed over the dead. On the southern side of the die, a figure in relief, of beautiful workmanship, by Launitz, represents her bereaved warrior, attempting to hide, while he betrays his grief. Upon another side is the record of her parentage:

DO-HUM-ME,

DAUGHTER OF

NAN-NOUCE-PUSH-EE-TOE,

A CHIEF OF THE SAC INDIANS.

A third side is thus inscribed:

DO-HUM-ME,

WIFE OF

COW-HICK-KEE,

A YOUNG WARRIOR OF THE IOWAS.

Upon the fourth side is the following inscription:

Died

IN NEW YORK,

MARCH 9TH, 1843,

AGED 18 YEARS.

"Thou'rt happy now, for thou hast past
The cold, dark journey of the grave;
And in the land of light at last,
Hast join'd the good, the fair, the brave."

SKETCH OF DO-HUM-ME.

BY MRS. C. M. SAWYER.

Do-HUM-ME, as her monument briefly sets forth, was the daughter of a chieftain of the Sacs, and the wife of a young war-chief of the Iowas. But from the obscurity which always, to a certain extent, rests over the history of individuals of savage nations, her biography, with all the aids which have been obtained from those who knew her, must necessarily be but a meager outline.

Of her childhood little is known, save that its one great bereavement, the death of her mother, left her, at the early age of seven years, cut off from all that watchful care, those tender endearments, which make childhood so happy, and which none but a mother knows so well how

INDIAN MOUND.   21

to render.   But He who seeth the wants of the lowliest of his children,
knoweth also how to provide for them; and He awoke in the breast of
the remaining parent of Do-hum-me, a strange, subduing tenderness,
which to the Indian warrior is all unwonted; and the heart of the stern
old chief, whose necklace numbered more scalplocks than that of any
other of his tribe, grew soft as a woman's, when he looked upon his
motherless child, until even the hunting-path and the council-fire were
forgotten for her sake.   No toil was too exhausting, no sacrifice too
great to be endured for her.

Thus, under the eye of paternal watchfulness, Do-hum-me, silently
as the flowers of her own bright prairies, sprang up to womanhood.
Possessing in an uncommon degree those traits of beauty most prized
by her race—ever gentle and good-humored—she was the idol of her
father, and the favorite of her tribe.   Monotonous and uneventful her
life must necessarily have been until her eighteenth year, when a new,
and, as it eventuated, fatal era occurred in her existence.

Prompted partly by a desire of adjusting some land difficulties at
Washington, partly by a curiosity to behold the great cities of the
white men, and partly by the artful and interested representations of the
designing and needy, a delegation of the Sacs and Iowas came to the
determination of visiting our Atlantic shores.   Do-hum-me, under her
father's care, with two other females much older than herself, one of
whom was a niece of the celebrated Black-hawk, accompanied them.

During their journey from the Far West, an affection sprang up between the youthful subject of this sketch and a young chief of the
Iowas, which soon ripened into an intimacy ending in marriage.   The
interesting ceremony which united them, was performed at Paterson,
according to their own rites, and in the presence of their tribe, and a

6

number of white persons who had become interested by the beauty and amiable deportment of the youthful couple. Soon after their marriage they arrived in New York, where they attracted great attention, not less by their beauty and gracefulness, than by their undisguised affection for one another. They were never separated;—proud of each other, loving and happy, the animated smile of the bridegroom, and the gay, musical laugh of the bride, were a joy to all beholders. Gifts were showered upon them from all quarters, and the jewelry of Do-hum-me might have been coveted by many a fairer-hued bride.

But a dark cloud arose on the horizon of their wedded bliss, and their marriage-torch went suddenly out in darkness. Unaccustomed alike to the luxuries of civilized life, which by well-meaning but mis-judging friends were too lavishly heaped upon them, and the whirl and bustle by which they were continually surrounded, Do-hum-me sudden-ly fell a victim to her new and false position. A violent cold, contracted one stormy evening to which they were exposed, superadded to indis-position produced by the causes already alluded to, at once assumed the alarming character of inflammation; congestion ensued, and in a few brief hours, all was over.

Thus died Do-hum-me, a stranger, and in a strange land. Far away from all familiar things and places, in a little more than four weeks from her bridal, she passed to her burial. Almost deserted in her death, —for the two females who had accompanied her from her home had already found a grave, the one dying in a hospital of Philadelphia, the other but three weeks before in New York,—and the thousands who had come around them to gaze and wonder, at the rumor of a conta-gious disease having broken out among the hapless company, had without exception taken flight,—one only of her own sex, whose sympathies were stronger than all fear, stood by her side, to administer to her wants, to soothe her last moments, and to close her eyes when all was over.

An attempt to describe this last sad scene, would be utterly futile. The helpless bewilderment—the agony, almost despair, of the doting father and husband—their piteous wails and sobs—the irrepressible tears which, unwiped, flowed down their dusky cheeks, altogether formed a picture which can never be forgotten, and which forever disproves the oft-told tale of the Indian's coldness and stoicism.

In the same gay ornaments with which, with a girlish pride, De-hum-me had adorned herself for her bridal, she was again decked for the grave; and it was with no other feeling than that of reverence and grief, that the hand of civilization aided that of the savage, in braiding the dark locks, and circling the neck of the bride of death, with the sparkling chain and gay and flashing gem. She was followed to her last resting-place by those dearest to her in life, as well as by that friend whom Providence directed to her bedside in the last bitter hour of dissolution. There, in a spot aptly chosen for the grave of the forest-girl, she reposes in the last, dreamless slumber. She hears not the ocean-winds that sigh around her green-roofed dwelling; the footsteps of the frequent pilgrim disturb her not;—for, let us believe that, according to her own simple faith, her spirit is lovingly, patiently waiting, in some far-off but happy sphere, till those she so loved on earth shall join her, never more to be separated.

THE FOREST-CHILD.

BY MRS. SAWYER.

By the banks of Sylvan Water,
  Where the Green-Wood shadows rest,
Sleepeth Iowa's young daughter,
  In a mournful mother's breast!
In a mother's breast that never
  Groweth harsh, or stern, or cold,—
Lock'd in arms that will forever
  Tenderly their child enfold!

Summer winds above her sighing,
  Softly kiss the drooping flowers;
Summer rains, like lutes replying,
  Make sweet music to the hours!
Winter snows, around her falling,
  Robe the dell, the copse, and hill;
Spirits through the storm are calling—
  But the maiden sleepeth still!

In a far-land, where the prairie,
  Stretch'd in boundless beauty, lies,
Lovely as a woodland fairy,
  Open'd she at first her eyes;
Many a sweet flower, round her springing,
  Gladness to her bosom lent;
Many a bright bird o'er her winging,
  With her own its carol blent!

Eyes that watch'd her sinless childhood,
  Brighter beam'd when she appear'd,
Hearts that braved for her the wildwood,
  Toil or peril never fear'd!
Thus, with sky and forest o'er her,
  Grew to maidenhood the child,
While the light of love before her,
  On her path in beauty smiled!

INDIAN MOUND.

From that far-land came she hither;
　Hearts long loved were by her side;
But we saw her fade and wither,
　Till, like summer flowers, she died!
To her sylvan couch we bore her,
　When the twilight shadows fell;
Softly smooth'd the green turf o'er her,
　Where in death she slumbers well!

Stricken bride! amid the places
　Thou didst love, thy grave should be,—
Here, of all the pale-hued faces,
　Who, save one, has wept for thee!
Lo! I hear a sound of anguish
　From the far Missouri's shore—
'Tis the voice of those who languish,
　That they see thy face no more!

There thy sire all lowly sitteth,
　Weeping sadly and alone;
There thy hunter still forgetteth
　Those that live for one that's gone!
Peace be round their lonely pillow,
　In that far-off, western wild!
Thou, beside the ocean-willow,
　Sweetly sleep, poor Forest-child!

7

BAY-GROVE HILL.

"The city bright below; and far away,
    Sparkling in golden light, his own romantic bay.

*   *   *   *   *

Tall spire, and glittering roof, and battlement,
    And banners floating in the sunny air;
And white sails o'er the bright blue waters bent;
    Green isle, and circling shore, are blended there,
In wild reality."

Two of the plates in this number are representations of tombs situated near the summit of Bay-grove Hill. The material, the elaborate execution, and more than all, the commanding position of these structures, make them particularly prominent and attractive. The beautiful eminence which they occupy, is not far from the entrance. The view from this spot will detain the visitor a moment. An opening on his left reveals to him the lower bay, Staten Island, and the Narrows. Another, in front, reaches across the harbor, and is bounded by the masts, spires, and dwellings of New York and Brooklyn. The little dell which he has just passed, with its shady water, is immediately below. Here, with a city of the living before him, and another of the dead growing up around, the charm of contrast is felt in its power. Here are presented, as it were, side by side, art and nature—bustle and repose—life and death;—while each quiet sail, moving but noiseless, seems a fit medium of communication between them.

DE WITT CLINTON.

"To scatter plenty o'er a smiling land,
And read their history in a nation's eyes."

The remains of DE WITT CLINTON repose temporarily in one of the tombs on Bay-grove Hill. They were laid here in the expectation that they would soon find a final resting-place in some commanding portion of the ground, and beneath a monument worthy of his great name, and of the city and commonwealth which owe so much to him. But this tribute to the memory and services of her most distinguished benefactor, New York has yet to pay. A beginning, indeed, has been effected by the proffer of a few liberal contributions, but no general and earnest call has yet been made. To such a call, this great and wealthy community will doubtless respond with its wonted liberality.

As this duty, which has too long remained unfulfilled, may soon be urged anew, a brief glance at the services and character of Clinton, may serve to remind some, and to inform others, of his pre-eminent claims to such commemoration.

DE WITT CLINTON was born 1769, at Little Britain, a small town in the pastoral valley of the Walkill. His grandfather, Charles Clinton, though of English descent, came to this country from Ireland, in 1729. At the capture of Fort Frontenac, during the French and Indian war, he was at the head of a regiment, while two of his sons, James, the father of De Witt, and George, afterward Governor of New York, and Vice-president of the United States, held subordinate commands. In the war of Independence, James Clinton was a general officer, and again did his country service.

Thus honored in his origin and connections, De Witt gave early promise of eminence on his own account. He was one of the first class graduated at Columbia College, after it was reopened subsequently to the Revolution. He studied law with the celebrated Samuel Jones, and in due course was admitted to the bar. At this conjuncture, his uncle, George Clinton, then Governor of New York, proposed to him to become his private secretary. Yielding his golden prospects in the law, to considerations of duty and gratitude, he accepted the place, and thus plunged at once into the restless sea of political life. Adopting, from conviction, the anti-federal opinions of his uncle, he defended them as a matter of duty; and it is highly creditable to his power as a writer, that he was thought by multitudes to maintain his ground, although his antagonists were the immortal authors of the "Federalist." From 1797 to 1801, he was a member of the state legislature, and the acknowledged leader of his party. He was opposed, generally, to the national administration of that period, but not with a bitter or undiscriminating hostility. In 1801, being only thirty-two years old, he was elected senator of the United States. In this august body, he at once took high rank as a statesman and debater. In 1803 he was appointed mayor of New York, and, with the exception of two years, continued to hold that responsible post until 1815.

By virtue of this office, as then constituted, he was the head of the city police, chief judge of the criminal court and common-pleas, and chairman of the board of health, with a large patronage at his sole disposal. In the discharge of these various and onerous duties, his course seems to have been uniformly firm, and able, and honest. During a large portion of the same period, he was also a member of the New York legislature. Though sharing largely in the political conflicts of those exciting times, he gave to objects of public and lasting utility, his great personal and official influence.

Statesmanship was, with him, no narrow, selfish policy, looking only to the advancement of individual interests, or the extension and consolidation of party power. To every scheme of benevolence and improvement, well intended and well devised, he lent his willing aid. The weather-beaten old sailor, resting at last in his "Snug Harbor," with the name of Randall may gratefully join that of Clinton, as having made secure to him his comfortable home. The Bloomingdale Asylum for the Insane was founded by grants, which Clinton proposed and carried. The first establishment in New York for the encouragement of the fine arts, obtained its charter through his agency, and was ever after an object of his care. Many instances of his benevolence and public spirit are of necessity omitted; but one great benefaction, belonging to this period of his life, must not be passed by. The Free School Society, which became the seminal principle and the nucleus of that great system of public instruction, by which the state now gives an education to her million of children, was devised by De Witt Clinton. By his exertions a charter was obtained—private subscriptions were secured—the city corporation was enlisted in its favor—and finally, a liberal grant was made by the state. How humble the beginning,—how magnificent the result! It may well be doubted whether even the far-reaching mind which conceived the plan, ever anticipated the mighty issue of this generous endeavor to provide free schools for the neglected children of New York. To every wise and well-meant effort for human improvement, this example is a perpetual voice of cheering and promise.

Though enough has been adduced in even these brief details, to show that De Witt Clinton might well rank among the great and good, it is not on these grounds that his renown chiefly rests. His attention seems to have been first turned to the subject of improving the internal

communications of New York, in 1809. Being at that time the acknowledged leader of the democratic party in the state senate, he was
invited by Judge Platt, who held the same position on the federal side,
to co-operate in procuring the appointment of a commission for exam-
ining and surveying the country between the Hudson and Lake Erie,
with reference to uniting these waters by a canal. He assented, and
these rival aspirants,—would that such spectacle might be oftener seen !
—rising above the selfishness and jealousies of party, joined heart and
hand in this great undertaking. In the following summer, as one of the
commissioners, he examined the entire route, and from that time, never
doubted the importance or feasibility of the work. In 1812, the prospects of the enterprise, which, up to that time, had been highly auspicious, were interrupted by the commencement of hostilities with
England. In 1815 the storm of war had passed away, but the position
of parties and of individuals was, in many instances, greatly altered.
The fluctuating tide of popular favor, on whose topmost wave Clinton
had so long ridden, had now subsided, leaving him stranded on the
shore. But though out of office—though discarded by the party which
he had served and led—he possessed still that better influence, which
high talent, well and steadily devoted to the public good, never fails to
acquire. This soon became manifest. He drew up a memorial, ex-
hibiting the practicability and usefulness of the proposed canal ; the
expediency of constructing it, though it should yield no revenue ; the
probable cost, and the unquestionable ability of the state to meet it.
Its lucid statements and convincing argument, carried conviction everywhere. Its presentation to the legislature was soon followed by the
act of 17th April, 1816, "to provide for the improvement of the internal navigation of the state." He was appointed one of the five com-

missioners constituted by this act, and entered forthwith upon the work.

The star of Clinton was clearly again in the ascendant. The office of governor having become vacant in 1817, he was raised to the chair by a vote nearly unanimous. The change was wonderful. Old party lines could no longer be found. The golden age had returned. Such was the pleasing dream of many who beheld the treacherous calm. But not then, assuredly, had parties in New York acquired the graceful art,

" To rise with dignity, with temper fall."

The sweet harmony of consenting voices, which had so lately charmed all ears, was soon changed to harsh discord. Discontents arose. New combinations of party were formed. Governor Clinton and his measures were strongly opposed. Even the canal was not spared. Faction, in its frothy violence, could find for this most magnificent of human enterprises, no worthier designation than that of " the big ditch."

From this acrimonious contest Clinton came out victorious, but with a diminished majority. His second term of office was one protracted battle. A majority of the legislature was unfriendly. His political opponents were able, as well as numerous and active. Weary, at length, of the unprofitable struggle and thankless honor, he declined a third trial, and retired to private life.

During all these fluctuations of the political world, the canal, that great object of his care and ambition, went steadily forward. His able and unpaid services as senior commissioner, had been devoted to the work through its whole progress. Yet in 1824, when it was nearly completed,—when it had already become a source of revenue to the state, and of unexampled prosperity to the regions which it traversed, and those which it connected, Clinton, to whom this great success was almost wholly due, was removed by a legislative vote, from his place as canal commissioner. No want of capacity or fidelity was, or could be alleged. Not even a pretext was assigned. It was the sovereign act of politicians in power, mistaking, for the moment, the character and sentiments of a great people. No leading-strings of party could drag them to approve what seemed a manifest injustice. The indignation was general. Clinton was immediately put in nomination for the chief magistracy; and his election by an overwhelming majority, assured him that gratitude and honor yet survived.

In October, 1826, the final completion of the Erie canal was celebrated with great rejoicings. It is easier to conceive than to describe the emotions which must have swelled the heart of Clinton, during that long, triumphal voyage from Buffalo to New York, when the virgin Nereid of our great inland seas was conducted to her bridal with the Ocean-king. It was the consummation of that enterprise to which, for more than fourteen years, he had consecrated his time and strength, his pen and voice. To effect it, he had endured not only anxiety and fatigue, but even obloquy and proscription. Now, with evidence so ample that, at last, those exertions were widely and deeply appreciated, the measure of his actual fame might well fill even his great ambition. And still he must have known that the benefits of the canal with which his name was now inseparably twined, had only begun to be felt. Rich as was the freight which it already wafted to the sea, its commerce was as yet but the mountain rivulet, which, swelled at length by a thousand tributaries, would roll on, a mighty tide, and freshen the Atlantic with its Amazon of waters.

DE WITT CLINTON. 33

His useful career was now approaching its close. Again elected to the chief magistracy, he entered on his last term of office in 1827. In the autumn of that year his health began to fail. His disease did not, however, prevent him from attending to his official and daily duties, down to the very hour of his departure, which occurred suddenly, February 15, 1828. No palsied energies, no streams of dotage, marked the closing scene. He was still high in station and respect;—still cheered by the gratitude and admiration of his countrymen;—full as ever of benevolent and sagacious plans and deeds—when the summons came. From that height of undiminished usefulness, of influence, and fame, he dropped into the tomb.

Twenty years have passed since Clinton died. Time, magic healer! has salved the wounds of political strife, and the sober light of historic truth, neither dimmed nor deflected by the mists of contemporary prejudice, shines at length upon his life and character. Interested partisans have ceased to lavish on his name praises not deserved, and disappointed enemies no longer denounce it.

That his abilities were of a high order, was perhaps never questioned. The well-contested fields of party strife,—the stations of honorable and laborious responsibility which he adorned and dignified,—the enterprises of broad and permanent usefulness which he achieved, establish the point. There have been ordinary men of popular and plausible talents, who have gained a short-lived reputation for greatness. Such was the case with some of Clinton's successful competitors for power and place. What are they now? Hardly can we say, "stat nominis umbra!" But Clinton was of another stamp. His ideas were vast, and his works, commensurate with the conceptions in which they originated, retain the impress of a master-hand. His re-

9

nown, accordingly, was no ephemeral growth. The tree, deep-rooted and wide-branching, while it has expanded and grown fairer in the air and sunshine, has also been tested and strengthened by the very blasts that have shaken it.

His mind was distinguished by its massive strength, rather than by variety or flexibility of power. It could grasp strongly subjects of high import and wide extent, retaining and revolving them, until it had mastered their minutest details. The cast of his intellect was decidedly practical. His imagination, if not naturally feeble, had lost its activity under early and habitual restraint. All the more, perhaps, was his judgment cool and discriminating. His untiring industry enabled him to bring to his investigations all that learning could contribute, while his power to analyze and recombine, helped him to turn those treasures to the most effective account. Hence the wisdom of his plans, and his almost prophetic anticipation of results. Hence he had none of the dreams of the mere visionary, nor the dazzling schemes of an enthusiast. How different might have been the issue of the canal enterprise in New York, had not the wild notions and specious eloquence of Gouverneur Morris been counteracted by the clear head, and strong good sense of De Witt Clinton! That vast project, which, under favorable auspices, became the boast and wonder of the age, might have perished, a still-born folly, or, if attempted, could have ended only in utter failure.

The wisdom which was so conspicuous in selecting the points to be connected, and the region to be traversed by the proposed canal, as well as in the plan and prosecution of the work, was even more signally manifest in that financial basis upon which, through the same influence, it was made to rest. To the exertions of Clinton, New York owes it, that, adopting the only honest and safe course in such matters, she has retained her credit as well as prosperity,—while other states, following the example of her improvements, but trusting to the income from their works, for the liquidation of their debts, have involved themselves in perplexing and discreditable embarrassment.

Though eminent as a statesman,—though unequalled in that ability which could devise and execute works of public and lasting benefit,—his merit was not confined to these departments. He had a strong predilection for scientific pursuits, and found time to investigate successfully some of the branches of natural history. His contributions on these subjects were made public, and still bear testimony to his zeal and assiduity. Of his talents as a writer, evidence remains not only in numerous state-papers, but in published addresses, delivered on literary and civil occasions. The style of his oratory seems to have partaken of the general character of his mind. He owed something to personal appearance, much to his weight of character, still more to the substantial merits of his discourse. His elocution, if not particularly graceful, was impressive and dignified.

Clinton's success as a political man, must be ascribed to higher merits than affability of manners, or the winning arts of the demagogue. In his public communications, and in social intercourse, where not closely intimate, his habits were stately and reserved. He had never studied in the school of modern non-committalism, nor would he seek, by an insinuating address, or by chicane and intrigue, the influence which argument and right had failed to gain.

In person he was tall and well-proportioned, while on his Roman brow and lip, as of one born to command, sat the firmness of self-possession, and the dignity of conscious power.

But it is when we contemplate Clinton as a man, faithful and true in every domestic and social relation;—as a patriot, self-sacrificing and devoted;—as a statesman and judge, virtuous and incorruptible;—as a benefactor to his own and coming times, rarely surpassed, that his name shines most brightly, and will be longest remembered. He was not, indeed, faultless. We recall with regret that devotion to party, which on the one hand, blinded him to the faults of his political friends, and on the other, made him sometimes unjust and uncharitable toward his opponents. Through his whole course we discern too much, perhaps, of that "sin, by which fell the angels."

But we must not forget the trying character of those times. The tides of party violence ran high. Besides that great strife which agitated the whole country, and shook the Union to its centre, New York, herself "imperium in imperio," was never without some fierce struggle of her own. Like Jupiter with his moons, she formed an entire, though subordinate planetary system, and her intestine perturbations were neither few nor small. To the political pilots of those stormy years let us forgive something, if their barks occasionally drifted with the currents which they undertook to stem.

Clinton's hostility as a politician, however severe, was not personal. To this point we have the testimony of one of his most illustrious antagonists. When the news of his decease reached Washington, the New York delegation in Congress held a meeting, to express their sense of the public loss. Mr. Van Buren, then of the senate, offered the resolutions, and paid the following tribute to his worth—a tribute which must have been as affecting as it is just and beautiful.

"I can," said Mr. V. B., "say nothing of the deceased that is not familiar to you all. To all he was personally known, and to many of us, intimately and familiarly from our earliest infancy. The high order of his talents, the untiring zeal and great success with which those talents have, through a series of years, been devoted to the prosecution of plans of great public utility, are also known to you all, and by all, I am satisfied, duly appreciated. The subject can derive no additional interest or importance from any eulogy of mine. All other considerations out of view, the single fact that the greatest public improvement of the age in which we live, was commenced under the guidance of his counsels, and splendidly accomplished under his immediate auspices, is of itself sufficient to fill the ambition of any man, and to give glory to any name. But, as has been justly said, his life, and character, and conduct have become the property of the historian; and there is no reason to doubt that history will do him justice. The triumph of his talents and patriotism, cannot fail to become monuments of high and enduring fame. We cannot, indeed, but remember, that in our public career, collisions of opinion and action, at once extensive, earnest, and enduring, have arisen between the deceased and many of us. For myself, sir, it gives me a deep-felt though melancholy satisfaction to know, and more so, to be conscious, that the deceased also felt and acknowledged, that our political differences had been wholly free from that most venomous and corroding of all poisons, personal hatred.

"But in other respects, it is now immaterial what was the character of those collisions. They have been turned to nothing, and less than nothing, by the event we deplore; and I doubt not that we shall, with one voice and one heart, yield to his memory the well-deserved tribute of our respect for his name, and our warmest gratitude for his great and signal services. For myself, sir, so strong, so sincere, and so engrossing is that feeling, that I, who, while he lived, never, no, never envied him any thing, now that he is fallen, am greatly tempted to envy him his grave, with its honors."

But there is other and better extenuation for the errors into which the heat of political conflict sometimes hurried this great man. Though a partisan of the warmest temperament, his devotion to party objects was never selfish. Whatever else may be said, he was not of that class of narrow men,

"Who to party give up what was meant for mankind."

To his praise be it remembered, that personal aggrandizement was not the ruling motive of his life. Though his official position gave him multiplied opportunities to enrich himself and his family, he resolutely scorned them all, and died as he lived, a rare example of Aristidean virtue. He contended earnestly for power, but it was the power to do good. He *was* ambitious, but it was ambition in its brightest phase, and scarcely can we find it in our hearts to chide the aspiring vice, which was so noble in purpose, and so beneficent in act.

Envy has sometimes denied the paramount merit of Clinton in the great enterprise of the Erie Canal. But the question is not, whether he first made the suggestion of a navigable communication between the lakes and the Hudson. It is a fact of historic certainty, that the adoption, the prosecution, and the accomplishment of that gigantic undertaking, were owing mainly to his convincing statements, his vast influence, and indomitable perseverance. What other man was there then, or has there been since, who would have accomplished the same! Who, that has watched the course of events in New York, and the fluctuations of party legislation on this very subject, the canal,—but may well question, whether, without the agency just named, it would

DE WITT CLINTON.

to this day have been begun? To Clinton, then, as an honored instrument in higher hands, be the praise awarded! Citizens of this imperial state, whose numerical power the canal has doubled, and whose wealth it has augmented in a ratio that defies estimation, cherish and perpetuate his name! You enjoy the rich fruits which his foresight anticipated, and his toils secured. Let him rest no longer in an undistinguished grave. True, a name like Clinton's cannot die! It is written on that long, deep line with which he channelled the broad bosom of his native state;—it is heard at every watery stair, as the floating burden sinks or rises with the gushing stream;—it is borne on each of the thousand boats that make the long, inland voyage;—and it shines, entwined with Fulton's, on all the steam-towed fleets of barges, which sweep in almost continuous train, the surface of the Hudson. But these are the traces of his own hand. It is your duty and privilege to record it too. Engrave it, then, in ever-during stone. Embody your sense of his merits in the massive pile. From the loftiest height of beautiful Green-Wood let the structure rise, a beacon at once to the city and the sea. Severe in beauty, and grand in proportions, it should be emblematical of the man and of his works. Such a monument will be a perpetual remembrancer of Clinton's name, and of his inappreciable services; and will stand for ages, the fit expression of your gratitude and of his glory.

OAKEN BLUFF.

"A voice within us speaks that startling word,
'Man, thou shalt never die!' Celestial voices
Hymn it unto our souls: according harps,
By angel fingers touch'd, when the mild stars
Of morning sang together, sound forth still
The song of our great immortality:
Thick clustering orbs, and this our fair domain,
The tall, dark mountains, and the deep-toned seas,
Join in this solemn, universal song.
Oh, listen ye, our spirits; drink it in
From all the air."

THE monument on Oaken Bluff is almost upon the woody brow of Sylvan Water. It is composed of the same beautiful brown stone as those on Ocean Hill, already described. Its style also is similar, although somewhat more pyramidal, from the greater breadth of base. The corners of the die, and the roof are enriched, and the latter is surmounted by an urn.

On the right is seen a tomb-front, of the same material. The detail is Roman, and the proportions are massive. A strong pier at each of the front corners, terminates in an urn of bold outline.

Both of these structures present an aspect of great solidity, and a promise of permanence, which will doubtless be made good. This rare but most important character they derive partly from form and material, and partly from the perfection of the masonry.

FERN-HILL.

"And those who come because they loved
  The mouldering frame that lies below,
Shall find their anguish half removed,
  While that sweet spot shall sooth their wo.
The notes of happy birds alone
  Shall there disturb the silent air,
And when the cheerful sun goes down,
  His beams shall linger longest there."

THE monument on Fern-Hill is an obelisk of unique character.
The outline diminishes from the base upward, in successive stages of
slight curvation, and the figure furnishes an agreeable variety in this
very popular class of sepulchral decorations.   The stone is a hard and
very dark sienitic or trap rock from Staten Island; it is polished
throughout,—and its entire aspect is impressive and becoming.   The
workmanship of this structure is admirable.   As in the old Athenian
masonry, the separate stones are so nicely adjusted, that they require
no intervening cement.   This obelisk occupies the centre of a large,
circular lot, and its position is commanding and beautiful.

MONUMENTS.

"Why call we, then, the square-built monument,
The upright column, and the low-laid slab,
Tokens of death, memorials of decay?
Stand in this solemn, still assembly, man,
And learn thy proper nature; for thou seest
In these shaped stones and letter'd tables, figures
Of life;
                                        —types are these
Of thine eternity."

THE establishment of rural cemeteries has awakened, by natural consequence, a livelier interest in the whole subject of sepulchral monuments. The feeling which prompts the erection of some memorial over the ashes of a friend, is undoubtedly a dictate of our common humanity. A great philosophic poet ascribes the custom to that consciousness of immortality, which he believes to be universal, and which is but aided and confirmed by the teachings of religion. Whatever the cause, its observance has marked every race and age in man's whole history, and appears not less in the "frail memorial," than in the gorgeous mausoleum; in the simple Indian mound, than in the "star-y-pointing pyramid." The supposed necessities of city life, or its poor and heartless conventionalities, alone have been able to check or divert for a time the expression of this spontaneous sentiment. But these interments in towns must be discontinued; and the expectation is not preposterous, that the crowded charnel-houses which have so long re-

MONUMENTS. 43

ceived the dead to loathsome crypts, and nameless oblivion, will soon be closed forever.

Well, then, may the introduction of the rural cemetery be hailed as the revival of a better taste, and the return to more healthy usages. It is something—it is much—to have transferred the resting-place of the departed from the blank and grim enclosures, the thoughtless and fierce turmoil of the city, to some retired and beautiful spot,—even though many continue to cling to their old associations, and, notwithstanding the necessity has ceased, still retain the tomb. " Dust thou art, and unto dust shalt thou return." How shall this inevitable condition be fulfilled most completely and naturally,—with the highest degree of safety to the living, and of security from desecration, to the dead ? The question, however various may be the practice, admits, it is believed, of but one answer. That answer is, by single interments in the free soil. Nature, reason, experience, utter the response, and taste reiterates and confirms it. To this conviction the public mind seems to be gradually, but surely coming. With the progress of this change, we witness an increasing attention to commemorative memorials, and evident improvement in their forms and modes of erection. Such improvement was greatly needed. Bear witness a thousand grave-yards, but too emblematic of decay and dissolution ! Witness ten thousand tablets, once bearing the names and virtues of the lamented dead, and fondly reared to their " memory," now mossy, mouldering, inclined, or prostrate, puzzling the groping visiter, and sometimes baffling even antiquarian patience ! Witness especially, those heaps unsightly of brick and mortar, formerly veneered with costly marble, now half denuded, or entirely fallen, with their recorded " hic jacet" doubly true. It is almost impossible to find a monument composed of several pieces united by masonry, which has stood twenty years, without more or less of dilapidation and displacement. This evil has been too palpable not to be widely felt, and the wonder is, that spectacles so discreditable should have been endured so long.

Of the beautiful cemeteries lately formed among us, we hope better things. That the hope be not delusive, will require untiring vigilance on the part of those who conduct these establishments, and the use of every precaution, by those who occupy the grounds. In the comparatively modern Père la Chaise, this evil has already become great, and even in some of the still more recent English cemeteries, is beginning to be matter of complaint. Climate, the main source of the difficulty, is probably not more favorable here than it is in France and England. We are subject to the extremes of heat and cold, of moisture and dryness; to intense frosts and sudden thaws. No material that can be used for monuments, has yet been found perfectly proof against these potent influences. But although there is not one, perhaps, of the stones in architectural use, which, exposed to the weather, is wholly invulnerable, it is certain that they differ widely in respect of durability. Ignorance or disregard of this fact has led to much of the decay and unsightliness which have so long characterized our places of sepulture. This is not, however, the only cause.

The whole subject of monumental erections, as a question both of taste and durability, must interest not only those who contemplate making such improvements in Green-Wood, but all who would preserve from deformities and desolation, a scene of unrivalled, and, as yet, undisfigured beauty.

Regarded as an affair of taste, the subject is one of some delicacy, and we venture upon it with becoming deference. We do not forget

MONUMENTS.

the right of each individual to have his own way in such matters, nor those maxims of universal currency, which rest upon the assumption, that in all this wide province there are no fundamental principles. We set up no invariable standard, nor would we, if in our power, enforce uniformity,—variety being essential to pleasing effect. But we have, notwithstanding, an unalterable conviction that all considerations of this sort rest upon certain laws of fitness and propriety, which cannot be violated, without a shock to every mind of just perceptions, and powers rightly cultivated. If it be a question of form only, the lines of beauty and deformity are not so easily decided. Yet even here there is less of latitude than is often supposed. There is a voice—the generally harmonious voice of cultivated taste. It has the sanction of numbers and of ages, and may not lightly be disregarded.

The simplest, cheapest form of sepulchral memorial, is the common head-stone. This, in its usual character of a thin tabular slab, merely inserted in the earth, is not allowed in Green-Wood, for the sufficient reason, that it cannot be made to retain an erect position. Particular graves are sometimes marked by tablets placed horizontally, and sometimes by thick stones at the ends, rising but a little from the surface. But the head-stone proper is not excluded. To give the required durability, it needs only be made sufficiently thick to rest firmly upon a well-supported base. This class of monuments is susceptible of many pleasing forms, and being modest and unexpensive, will be likely to suit the taste and means of not a few.

Of the more elaborate structures it will not be possible to treat in much detail. A few suggestions, of a general nature, will alone be attempted. In most of our rural cemeteries, the popular taste, ever prone to a servile imitation, has shown a strong predilection for pyramidic forms.

The chief objection is to the multiplication of one thing, producing, as it must, a wearisome sameness. We have seen a ground so full of pyramids and obelisks, that one could almost fancy it a gigantic cabinet of minerals, being all crystals set on end. But there are other considerations which should weigh in this matter. The great pyramid of Gizeh excites emotions of grandeur by its vast height and bulk. Reduce it to a model six feet high: the sublimity is gone, and there is no special beauty in the object to compensate for the loss. Those vast monolithal, acicular pyramids called obelisks, their summits piercing the skies, and their adamantine surfaces embossed with hieroglyphics, attract our gaze as marvels of patience and power. But what particular atoning charm have our petty and unsuccessful imitations of them, that they should usurp and fill so much space?

These remarks, it is scarcely necessary to add, urge not the exclusion of this class of monuments, but only a more sparing and sensible use of them. Set here and there among other diversified and graceful forms, these geometric solids might produce a happy effect. The dark conical fir-tree, judiciously planted amid masses of irregular and bright foliage, shows well in contrast, and pleases every eye. But who would fancy a park of firs?

Those whose hearts are set on pyramids and obelisks, will of course gratify that taste. While so doing, it may be well to remember, that in their angular measures, and in the relative dimensions of the monolith and pedestal, these seemingly monotonous structures differ very considerably,—often betraying, by their clumsiness, the bungling ignorance of those who designed them. In shape and proportions they should assuredly be consonant with the best forms of ancient art, unless indeed modern genius can improve upon those.

Among other antique forms still used, the sarcophagus and column are prominent. These are more susceptible of variety, and to lines of higher beauty, add the charm of classic associations. To the former of these, as a monument for the open air, it may perhaps be objected, that as commonlly placed, it is too low for impressive effect. Properly elevated on a massive base, it could scarcely fail to be imposing. To the simple pillar, likewise, as we usually see it, a similar objection holds. It is too slender; it lacks dignity; it does not fill the eye. To give it an effective diameter, would require a height which might be inconvenient or too expensive. The short rectangular pillar, or elongated pedestal, with regular base, die, and cornice, and supporting an urn, or some similar ornament, is a much more substantial object. This has been long in use among us, and seems to have been often resorted to, when it was proposed to have something particularly grand in the sepulchral line. Being executed generally in the style of mantel-work, the lines are for the most part rectilinear, meager in detail, and homely in expression. These monuments, with their brick cores and marble skins, are rapidly disappearing. Peace to their ruins! Let no presumptuous mortal attempt to reconstruct them!

But this kind of structure becomes a very different affair, when reared of solid material, and of stone, which yields to the chisel, and can defy the elements. Several monuments of this class, both square and tripodal, have been put up in Green-Wood, and have done much toward giving the improvements there a character for originality and beauty,—evincing, as they do, great capability, in the way of variety, of dignity, and of grace.

Numerous declivities in the grounds greatly facilitate the excavation and the use of tombs, and by consequence, render their fronts conspicuous. A cursory observation of the different entrances, is sufficient to show that there is, even in these humble façades, considerable scope as well as call for architectural skill. The conditions which we would see fulfilled, and which are actually attained here in many instances, are an appearance of perfect security and strength,—symmetrical proportions,—and that air of quiet solemnity, which becomes the entrance to a house of the dead.

The subject of monuments and devices strictly symbolical, opens a field for consideration, wider than we can now explore. Within the whole range of mortuary memorials, there is probably nothing which gives so complete satisfaction, as this embodiment of thought in marble speech, when it is felicitously conceived, and properly executed. Sculpture has won her greenest and most enduring crown, when, with mute eloquence, she tells the story of faith triumphant over mortal anguish,—and, with immortality written on her beaming brow, stands pointing heavenward. But in proportion to the greatness and gladness of that success which rewards the high endeavor, are the disappointment and disgrace which tread on the heels of failure. The eye of taste and the heart of sensibility are shocked by attempts, which convert into objects of ridicule and contempt, what ought only to solemnize and elevate the mind. In reference, then, to all original conceptions of a symbolic nature, the path of prudence seems plain. He who meditates a work of this description, ought surely to consider well before he decides, lest peradventure he record some expensive folly, in a material whose durability would then be its greatest misfortune. Such a work should bring into requisition the choicest talent and the highest skill. Genius and piety should furnish the design, and judgment and taste should superintend the task.

MONUMENTS. 49

For those who, in such matters, are content to copy the notions or works of others, the course is easier and safer. The public voice,— the voice, perhaps, of centuries,—may be considered as having passed sentence of approval on the forms which have been so often repeated or imitated. And yet how many even of these significant representations, fail to meet the demands of a chastened taste, or lack the sanction of reason and scripture. Angelic forms, for instance, have been favorite subjects of monumental sculpture. It could, indeed, hardly be otherwise. Our earliest and most cherished associations have accustomed us to blend some image of cherub or seraph, with every thought of the spiritual world. Sacred verse, from the nursery rhyme to the lofty epic, has made these winged messengers of heaven seem almost familiar to our senses. The Bible itself, through its whole course, from the sad, primeval hour, when

> "all in bright array,
> The cherubim descended,"

to close and guard the gate of Paradise, to that night of gladness, in which

> "sworded seraphim"
> Were "seen in glittering ranks, with wings display'd,
> Harping in loud and solemn quire,
> With unexpressive notes, to heaven's new-born heir;"—

is one continuous record of angelic visitations. In no way, perhaps, have the painter and sculptor more fully exhibited the power of genius and art, than in those happy efforts by which they have given to the eye these shapes of transcendent beauty and goodness. But such are the exceptions. Too often, these attempted personifications in stone, or on the canvass, do not even approach the bright conceptions with which poetry and inspiration have filled our imaginations. When the subject is thus elevated, nothing short of the highest attainment can satisfy our expectations; and with painful disappointment we turn away from the grotesque expression or incongruous attitude.

"Though sculptors, with mistaken art,
    Place weeping angels round the tomb,
Yet when the great and good depart,
    These shout to bear their conquerors home.

"Glad they survey their labors o'er,
    And hail them to their native skies;
Attend their passage to the shore,
    And with their mounting spirits rise.

"If, then, the wounded marble bear
    Celestial forms to grace the urn,
Let triumph in their eyes appear,
    Nor dare to make an angel mourn."

Of these imitations, the emblems most used are of Greek or Egyptian origin. To the dignity of age, some of them add that beauty of device and form, which Grecian genius could so well impart. No one can doubt that in their own time and place, these symbols were natural and appropriate, as well as beautiful. But are they so still? Seen among the cypresses of an Ionian cemetery, or over the ashes of some beloved and lamented Athenian youth, the fragmentary column, or the torch reversed and going out in darkness, was a fit expression of the popular belief, and truly symbolized a sorrow in which hope had neither lot nor part. To the mourners of pagan antiquity, death was extinction. To them, no voice from heaven had spoken. For them, no page of revelation shone. No seer divine had taught them those lessons of faith, which alone can give to the bereaved and sorrowing, assurance of immortality and reunion; when the broken pillar will be more than restored, and the extinguished blaze shall be relumined, never to fade again. With some reason might *they* plant upon the tomb, the tokens of crushed affections and hopeless grief. But when a Christian weeps for departed loveliness, or would raise some memorial for one who has died in the faith and peace of the gospel, are these the emblems which he should adopt? Shall he upon whose eye has beamed the star that first shed a radiance on the grave, and still lights up the once dark realms beyond, employ the same symbols with the pagan and the infidel? As a question of religious consistency—of simple propriety—of mere taste, even,—has this matter been sufficiently considered? We pretend not to suggest the forms which should either constitute or embellish the mementoes that rise for the dead in a Christian land. Happily there is no lack of those which are both beautiful and appropriate. They will readily be found by such as seek for them. Those who will use the gloomy hieroglyphics of some perished creed, should at least place near them the cheering emblems of a living faith. If Death be represented with downcast look and inverted flame, let Immortality, as in the fine group of Thorwaldsen, stand by his side, with torch high blazing, and eyes upturned in love and rapture.

A strong disposition has of late been prevalent, to revive, for civil, monumental, and religious purposes, the architecture of the ancient world. When man builds for his own accommodation, or for objects purely civil and secular, the questions which he is called to settle are those of utility and beauty mainly. But when he rears a temple to God, or a memorial for the dead, there are other considerations which demand a hearing. In determining the style of erections designed to express and to cherish emotions of tenderness and piety, it is not wise—it is not safe to disregard those influences which belong to associated thought, and to time-hallowed memories. We are creatures of sentiment and sympathy. A few, in their superior illumination, may profess indifference to the power of circumstances so trivial. But these are not "the people." However they may doubt or deny the reality, the world yet rolls on, and round,—and causes, not the less irresistible that they are unseen and despised, still move the rising and retiring tides of human passion.

It is in disregard of such influences as those above referred to, that some modern philanthropists have thought it a good speculation, both pecuniary and, religious, to purchase theatres, and convert them into houses of public worship. Has the experiment worked well? Not so did the early Christians. When Rome was converted from idolatry to the religion of the cross, thousands of temples were abandoned by their worshippers. Here were structures ready furnished to their hands. Did their Grecian symmetry—their pillars of polished marble and porphyry—their tesselated floors—or their magnificent cornices and colonnades—tempt the followers of Jesus within their walls? Nay, they knew too well the power of old associations, to set up a pure and spiritual worship, on pavements lately wet with libations to Bacchus and Venus,—where altars had smoked to Jupiter and Mars, —and where every familiar object must have been redolent of error and impurity. And is Christian architecture so poor and scanty,—is modern genius so sterile, that we must seek the models of our churches in "superstitious" Athens, and derive the forms of our sepulchral monuments, gateways, and chapels, from calf-adoring Egypt?

An American writer, who had noticed the strong predilection for

MONUMENTS.   53

the antique manifested in the oldest of our cemeteries, has happily expounded the principles of taste and feeling which should prevail in sepulchral architecture.   We quote from the North American Review for October, 1836 :

"It is very doubtful whether the Egyptian style is most appropriate to a Christian burial-place.   It certainly has no connection with our religion.   In its characteristics it is anterior to civilization ; and therefore is not beautiful in itself.   No one will deny the superiority of the Grecian in mere point of beauty.   But more than this, Egyptian architecture reminds us of the religion which called it into being,—the most degraded and revolting paganism which ever existed.   It is the architecture of embalmed cats and deified crocodiles : solid, stupendous, and time-defying, we allow ; but associated in our minds with all that is disgusting and absurd in superstition.   Now, there is certainly no place, not even the church itself, where it is more desirable that our religion should be present to the mind, than the cemetery, which must be regarded either as the end of all things,—the last, melancholy, hopeless resort of perishing humanity,—the sad and fearful portion of man, which is to involve body and soul alike in endless night ; or, on the other hand, as the gateway to a glorious immortality,—the passage to a brighter world, whose splendors beam even upon the dark chambers of the tomb.   It is from the very brink of the grave, where rest in eternal sleep the mortal remains of those whom we have best loved, that Christianity speaks to us, in its most triumphant, soul-exalting words, of victory over death, and a life to come.   Surely, then, all that man places over the tomb should, in a measure, speak the same language.   The monuments of the burial-ground should remind us that this is not our final abode : they should, as far as

14

possible, recall to us the consolations and promises of our religion."

For the highest class of monumental tributes, we must resort to the studio of the sculptor. Personal representations, whether real or allegorical, will ever maintain in the world of art a superiority to all other forms, not unlike that which belongs to their prototypes in the worlds of life and thought. Accordingly, in all ages and lands in which art has flourished, monumental sculpture has abounded. In our busy country, the era of the fine arts, if in progress, has but just begun. As was to be expected, our patronage of the brush and chisel thus far has been somewhat characteristic, if not selfish,—amounting to little more than orders for portraits and busts, to adorn the domestic halls which still rejoice in the presence of the originals. Nor is it because they could not be had, that better things have not been more generally sought. In the first of these departments American genius has for years been distinguished; and in the latter, it has entered on a career which promises to be long and brilliant. To native merit of so high order, our countrymen cannot long remain insensible and unjust. With increasing wealth and leisure,—with advancing knowledge and refinement,—with travel more frequent and extended, the patronage of art will undoubtedly keep pace. In that coming and not distant age of Phidian splendor, the dead will claim and receive no inconsiderable share of the sculptor's skill. Wealth, refined by taste, and quickened by the promptings of grief and affection, will delight to preserve in breathing marble the loved form which has faded from earth. Through the medium of this most expressive art, the language of sorrow and of hope may be conveyed to the eye with happiest effect; and while propriety in design might thus go, hand in hand, with sensibility of feeling, merit would reap a fostering reward. Large sums have not unfrequently been devoted to the erection of huge Egyptian monuments,—to fanciful tombs below and above ground,—or to piles of masonry, which, beyond their expensiveness, have little or nothing else to boast of. Had these ample means been applied to secure works of high art from a Greenough or Power, a Crawford or Brown, how different the result, both as to present effect and enduring influence!

For all purposes of improvement in the arts—of national reputation —of patronized genius, need we say that the former are utterly inefficient? Were there, on the other hand, in the grounds at Green-Wood, a single perfect statue—but one great master-piece of American sculpture, to be seen and studied by the myriads who annually visit the spot, can any one estimate the elements of power which would sit enthroned within its fair proportions?—power to awaken or enhance a sensibility to beauty,—power to elevate while it refines the intellect, and thus with reflex influence to aid in moulding the manners and the heart?

But there is one serious obstacle to the introduction of fine sepulchral statuary, which meets us at the threshold. Only one material, if we may believe the concurring voice and practice of artists in all ages, is suitable for the highest efforts of the chisel. But to expose under the open sky, and to all the rigors of our Scythian climate, the snowy marble on which months or years of labor have been expended, seems to be little less than barbarous. Those who have observed the effects of exposure in this country, upon even the hardest and purest of the Italian marbles, need not be told in how short a time weather-stains, and cracks, and exfoliation, do their ruinous work. If, then, we are ever to have in our cemeteries these noblest and most beautiful of all sepulchral memorials, some safe and becoming shelter must be provided for them.

The need of a chapel in Green-Wood, for the accommodation of those who would prefer to have some religious service on the ground, has been felt from the first. Nothing, it is supposed, but expenses deemed still more exigent, have prevented the government of the Institution from erecting, ere this, such a structure. Whatever of cogency there may have been in these reasons, it is respectfully suggested whether the chapel be not now the first and highest want of the Cemetery. When the great number of interments made in it is considered, it cannot be doubted, that there are many families, summoned by these mournful errands to the grave, to whom such a building would be a great accommodation. Nowhere, certainly, could the last rites of love and religion be more decently paid, than in such a place, set apart for funereal purposes; while, at the same time, the afflicted home might be relieved from what is too often the intrusive bustle of a crowded funeral. A cemetery chapel might also, we believe, be greatly useful, by furnishing a place where the friends of the deceased could, at the appointed hour, privately assemble; removing thus the supposed necessity of providing a long train of carriages,—a custom which involves much idle parade, and not unfrequently an oppressive expense.

But not to dwell on considerations which deserve a separate discussion, let us return to the thought which brought the chapel before us. The idea of using the structure proposed to be erected for burial services, to receive, also, and preserve delicate statuary and reliefs, was suggested in an article appended to a published statement of the Comptroller for 1845. The considerations then suggested have lost none of

MONUMENTS.

their weight. Already may be seen upon the ground sculpture of exquisite delicacy, seeking, as it were, the protection which it cannot find. The plan of a chapel for Green-Wood should be of a magnitude commensurate with the future prospects of this great institution. But the whole is not required at first, and we cannot permit ourselves to doubt, that a wing or portion of the needed fabric will soon adorn the ground.

Allusion was made, in the beginning of this essay, to the perishable nature of some of the materials used for monuments, and to the influence of atmospheric changes upon them all. This point has received less attention than its importance merits. Strength and durability are indeed proverbial attributes of stone; but they are possessed, by the numerous varieties in use, in widely-differing degrees. In the United States, stone has not been employed for architectural purposes either so long, or in such variety, as to furnish the means of deciding the question of comparative durability, though something may be learned from even our limited experience. In the old world the case is different. There the influences of time and weather have been fully tested. In the serene skies of southern Europe and of western Asia, may be seen many a marble pillar, over which two thousand winters have swept, without leaving a spot on their virgin purity, or dimming their original polish. But how unlike to this are the effects of northern skies! A few years since, an obelisk brought from Luxor in Egypt, was set up in the French capital. The material is a granite of almost impracticable hardness, and its highly-wrought pictured surfaces had suffered no injury from thirty centuries of African exposure. Already it has been found necessary to cover its sides with coatings of caoutchouc, to preserve them from the corrosive influence of a Parisian atmosphere. In England, the defacement of many stone structures from dilapidation gradually going on, has long been a subject of remark. A Report, which was made to the Commissioners of Woods and Forests, on occasion of selecting the stone for the new Houses of Parliament, gives minutely the history and character of all the principal building-stones of Great Britain. The results of the investigation were remarkable. They show that while some kinds of sand-stone and of lime-stone—the materials chiefly used in that country—have stood for seven or eight centuries, almost or quite uninjured, there are other varieties of the same minerals, which show signs of decay, after the lapse of as many years. In several ancient structures, where two sorts of stone were used, one of them has crumbled like so much wood, while the other continues in good preservation. Everywhere it was found that the growth of lichens on the surface of the stone, however it may disfigure its appearance, is favorable to its duration. The wide and thorough examination thus made, ended in the recommendation of a crystalline, magnesian lime-stone, or dolomite, as having given, on the whole, the best evidence of enduring value. The use of stone, as a building material, is fast increasing in our country,—and the facts in this Report are, so far as American quarries correspond to those of England, of the highest importance.

In the selection of a material for sepulchral purposes, regard should be had both to looks and durability. The adoption of a dark or a light tint, will naturally be determined in part by the style and position of the monument—in part by the taste of the proprietor. White, or something which approaches to it, has many admirers. When fresh it has an air of purity and brilliance, and contrasts happily with surrounding verdure. But, unfortunately, under our changeful and weeping skies, this beauty is soon tarnished. The fact will, undoubtedly, tend more and more to diminish the use of lime-stone and marble, unless some variety should hereafter be found, with powers of resistance and endurance superior to any known at present.

Among the harder and older rocks—granite, sienite, &c.—there are, doubtless, varieties which will satisfy every reasonable demand on the score of duration. These unyielding materials are entirely unsuited to structures distinguished by curvilinear forms, and carved ornaments, —and nothing can be better adapted than they are to those which are marked by rigid outlines of massive strength and time-defying solidity.

But one more stone requires a notice here. Of American sand-stones there is a large variety, from those which are so coarse and friable as to be neither good-looking nor lasting, to those which are fine-grained, compact, beautiful, and, in all probability, enduring also. Of this last description, is the red sand-stone, from New Jersey, to which allusion has more than once been made in the preceding numbers of this work. The quarry, which is at Little Falls, near Newark, was first opened for the erection of Trinity Church, in New York. In that elaborate edifice, which is built wholly of this material, it is wrought into every possible form of beauty and strength. The finest monuments and tomb-façades in Green-Wood are from the same source. It consists of quartz and mica united firmly by an argillaceous cement, and slightly colored with oxide of iron. The fineness and uniformity of its grain, its comparative hardness and great compactness, justify the belief that it will long resist the disintegrating energies of our varying climate. Should this prove the case, it will, as a material for monumental and architectural purposes, combine an assemblage of virtues, which belong to no other stone that has yet come into use among us.

But the finest of models, and the choicest of materials, will avail little, unless the foundation and erection be made with care. The monument should rest on a bed of concrete, extending below the action of frost and the grave-digger. Each stone should, if possible, reach quite across, leaving no vertical joints,—and, if stratified, it should invariably be laid so that the planes of lamination shall be horizontal. The best of waterproof cement should alone be used as a binding material; and it is still better to make the contiguous surfaces so true as to require only an intervening sheet of lead. With the careful use of such precautions, perpendicularity and permanence, for a long time to come, may be safely guarantied against all the ordinary causes of displacement and decay.

LAWN-GIRT HILL.

"And sweetly secure from all pain they shall lie,
    Where the dews gently fall, and still waters are nigh;
    While the birds sing their hymns, amid air-harps that sound
    Through the boughs of the forest-trees whispering around,
    And flowers, bright as Eden's, at morning shall spread,
    And at eve drop their leaves o'er the slumberer's bed!"

THIS beautiful knoll occupies a position in the Cemetery ground, very nearly central. It is a gentle eminence of oval shape. From its wood-crowned summit one looks out upon smooth lawns of sunny brightness. To the visiter approaching it from the east by the principal avenue, the view cannot fail to be pleasing. The warm cleared grounds are hedged in by the surrounding copse-wood, while here and there a vista invitingly opens,—and one, in particular, beautifully terminates in the waters of the Bay. A neat iron paling surrounds the hill, marking it as the appropriated final home of a large family.

THE TOUR,

FROM OCEAN HILL.

"I now shall be peopled from life's busy sphere;
Ye may roam, but the end of your journey is here.
I shall call! I shall call! and the many will come
From the heart of your crowds, to so peaceful a home;
The great and the good, and the young and the old,
In death's dreamless slumbers, my mansions will hold."

THE plate presents one of those views of quiet beauty which are so numerous in the grounds of this cemetery. The spectator stands among the trees on the sharp, western side of Ocean Hill. A glade of considerable extent is spread out before him. Its waving border is darkly fringed with foliage,—while its gentle declivities of various inclination lie warm and bright in the broad eye of day. The Tour, winding round in serpentine length and slowness, is lost finally in the distant copse. The whole character of the landscape accords perfectly with the spirit of the place. Here are rural beauty and repose. No human dwelling is within view, if we except the still mansions of the dead. Neither sight nor sound is here to remind us of the noisy, living world. Not unfrequently the long funereal train, moving on with the slow pace of wo, and with phantom-like stillness, gives the picture a melancholy but finishing touch.

SYLVAN CLIFF.

A mansion! rear'd with cost and care,
Of quaint device and aspect fair.
Its walls in rocky strength secure,
Its massive portal fast and sure:
And, all intrusion to foreclose,
Reclining near in grim repose,
Two guards canine forever wait,
Cerberean warders of the gate.
Hold fast, ye stones, your treasured clay,
Though wasting ages roll away;
Cling closely round the honor'd trust,
Nor yield one particle of dust!
Yet ye shall hear a voice at last,
Quaking beneath a clarion-blast!
Your dead shall hear that voice and rise,
And seek, on angel-wings, the skies!

A MONUMENTAL tomb in the early English style of Gothic architecture. The material is the New Jersey sand-stone, from the quarry at Little Falls. Its roof rests upon an arch, and is covered with stone tiles, cut and laid diamond-wise. The front is gabled, and a quatrefoil in relief, on the stone door, bears the date of erection. The apex of the gable is enriched by a bold finial. At each corner is a supporting buttress,—and the sides are still further sustained by walls that keep up the earth.

This tomb occupies a commanding position in the Tour, being on the high bluff over Sylvan Lake. This is one of the earliest tomb-fronts, of decided architectural character, erected on the grounds. It has attracted particular notice, as a new style for such erections. A blending of strength with beauty—an air of solemnity and repose—pervade the structure, and render it impressive.

NEW YORK PUBLISHED BY R. MARTIN

VISTA HILL.

"Yet not to thine eternal resting-place,
Shalt thou retire alone; nor couldst thou wish
Couch more magnificent."

VISTA HILL is a gentle elevation, situated on the Tour, in the immediate vicinity of Cedar Grove. A portion of this hill is enclosed by an iron paling, with a handsome gateway opening to the east. The spacious enclosure is slightly elliptical. This beautiful spot has been secured and set apart for burial purposes, by the Church of the Saviour. We have already had occasion to allude to this wise and Christian appropriation. Is it not wise to bind more closely together, by the solemn and tender associations of the grave, those who meet and worship in the same sanctuary? And is not that a heaven-born charity, which not only remembers the poor while living, but, with delicate regard to the tenderest feelings of our nature, provides for them *such* sepulture? Praise to those who designed, and who have accomplished the work!

One or two other congregations own lots in Green-Wood, but no other one has appropriated and enclosed a tract for common occupancy. The Cemetery still contains spots admirably adapted to such a use. Will not some, will not many of the two hundred churches, which are destined to make Green-Wood their place of burial, take care to secure these choice positions, before they shall be preoccupied by individual proprietors? That every church should have its own burying-ground, is consonant as well to natural fitness and religious propriety, as to long experience. The dead may indeed no longer rest under or around the sacred walls which were so dear to them in life. Yet the place of sepulture may be hallowed by solemn assembly and religious rite. As pastor and people—the young and the old—the rich and the poor, cluster together there, how precious, how holy will the place become! What more can it need to consecrate and endear it, than its own simple charms, associated, as they will then be, with so many treasures of the heart,—so many tender memories and consolatory hopes?

The enclosure on Vista Hill was consecrated in the presence of a large assembly, on the 18th September, 1845. A mild autumnal day gave additional beauty and interest to the scene, and to the services. From the address delivered on this occasion by the pastor, Rev. Mr. FARLEY, we have been permitted to make the following extracts:—

"And I rejoice especially that it is here,—here, among these verdant groves, and lawns, and solemn shades. How surprising it seems, that in some of the older parts of our country, among a people by no means wanting in the warm and deep affections of our nature, we can find so many instances where 'the bleak hill-side,' or 'bare common, without shrub or tree,' is the spot selected as the burial-place of the dead!—nay, more: where no care is given to replacing the falling headstones, or repairing the decaying tombs, or even the broken fences!

"I admit that, despite these apparent and sad intimations of neglect, the memory of the dead is there cherished with as much sensibility, at least, as ever prompted the erection of the costliest mausoleum, or planted and watched the 'forget-me-nots' and 'immortelles,' as they bloomed by the graves of the departed. But affection is not exhausted or weakened, by giving to it expression, nor the fount of feeling dried up, by embodying its appropriate signs; and for one, I confess to a good deal of reverence and tender regard, not only for the memory of the dead, but for the perishing body—the fleshly tabernacle in which the immortal spirit had sojourned.

"In that, I see the signet of the great and divine Architect, as well as on that which inhabited it. It is the dictate of nature to love it. We press it to our arms when living; we seal it with our kisses when dead. The dear who are absent, come to our imaginations in the hour of revery and solitude, clothed in the material forms which are so familiar; and in them are the dead who have been buried, remembered. Nay, when we think of them in that higher home, to which our Christian faith points us, in those spiritual bodies of which the Apostle speaks, whatever else be our ideas, the same eye seems to beam on us, the same smile to lighten the same features, the same hand to beckon us on. Hence, we find the remains of the dead sacred among all people; the violation of the grave, everywhere regarded as sacrilege. Hence, our complacency at seeing a portion of the wealth which is lavished on palaces for the living, appropriated to provide for, and fitly adorn the habitations of the dead. Honor, reverence, affection, we would say, then, to that curious, wondrous, beautiful mechanism of God, the body, when it has fulfilled its office! Glad let us be to lay it in the virgin soil of this fair spot! Soft fall the rays of the rising and setting sun, as they shine upon the green turf which covers it! The grateful shade of these noble trees, the odor and beauty of sweet flowers, shall add their fragrance and loveliness to the place; and whatever monument, or stone, or marble, may hereafter be raised here, we will find our plea for doing it, in the natural and strong promptings of the heart. But beyond this, there are high moral uses to be found in the place of graves, where that is well-selected and well-ordered. It is not only grateful to the mourner in the early freshness of grief, but may be full of blessed influences to all the living. I am strongly tempted to say, that whoever can come to such a place as this where we stand, and the entire Cemetery to which it belongs, and not be impressed, and impressed deeply, by these influences, must be largely wanting in the common seriousness of our nature. I know not the place which unites in its natural aspect, and in its great capabilities, more fitness at once for the main design for which it was chosen, and more fulness of material for instructive and useful lessons to the living, as the dwelling-place of the dead, than this fair domain. All that is needed to this latter end is, that when we come here, we surrender ourselves, in a suitable frame of mind, to the spirit of the place. And for this, I do not think it necessary that we should enter it always in the funeral train, when the passing bell, solemn and touching as it is, chimes out its requiem to the departed. It is enough that the place is set apart and secured, as far as human contrivance and law can go, for the purposes of a Cemetery, that is, as the word imports, a sleeping or resting-place for the dead.

"In its singular quiet, presenting a striking contrast to the noise and stir of the great cities close by; in its easy access, yet secluded position, almost washed by the solitary sea; in its diversified surface of hill and dale, glen and plain, woodland and copse, land and water; in its exquisite natural beauties, and its large extent, it is remarkably fitted in itself for these purposes. As year after year passes, and more and more of the living who have been accustomed to thread its avenues, are gathered within its bosom; as art and affection, from generation to generation, shall combine to do honor to the dead, rich and most affecting to the soul rightly disposed, will be the associations which shall cluster around it. And then to pause amid its still shades and think :— Here, indeed, is the place of the dead! The dust which the living have worn, is here mingling again with the dust. As years come and go, here will be gathered more and more, 'the mighty congregation of the dead.' The voice of spring will be heard in the gentle breeze, or the blast of winter will wail among these then naked branches, with every opening or dying year, long after the thousands who now throng the streets of yonder cities, shall have gone to swell its ranks!

"What a lesson is here read to us, by every little mound of earth that marks the bed of a sleeper, every monument that tells his name, on the folly and vanity of all human designs! Could the dead that lie buried within these graves, now rise and speak to us, how sobered should we find the tongue of frivolity; how careless of human fame the ambitious; how weak the passionate; how serious the worldling and the fop; how humble and sincere the proud and the pretender!

"There is another lesson to be learned here; and that relates to what survives, and is imperishable. The monuments of departed heroes, in the groves of the Academia, without the walls of the City of Minerva, would not permit Themistocles to sleep, so did the thought of their great deeds fire his soul! How much more should the place of the Christian dead, stir and wake us, as we pause amid its shades, to a holy emulation of their high and more than heroic graces! What

has passed, or is now passing away, is daily of less and less importance,—while what remains is imperishable.

"The affections are immortal. The reunion of Christian friends
after death, is a truth sanctioned by the entire teaching and spirit of the
Gospel. Every virtue which graced the character of the departed;
every pure wish and holy purpose; every sincere and holy prayer;
every disinterested, honest, generous deed,—all that really endeared
them to our hearts, are now like garlands of amaranth upon their
tombs, and cannot die. The baptism of death has put them beyond
the reach of temptation and sin. And when we stand by the spot
where their dust reposes, we seem adjured, in tones that pierce the
soul, by motives too mighty to be resisted, to be good, pure, faithful,
even unto death, that when we too come to die, we, like them, may
rest from our labors, and our good works follow us.

"Ever sacred, then, be this spot to the pious uses for which it is set
apart! Ever precious in presence and in memory, to the mourner!
Ever blessed and subduing in its influences and associations, to the
prosperous and the happy! May it serve, dearly beloved, as a new
bond to keep us together, a united and Christian flock! Whenever
our feet bend their way hither, either to perform the last offices of
Christian affection and piety, or to strengthen our spirits amid the
sober meditations which befit the place, and are inspired by it, may
we, one and all, be prompted to an increased fidelity to the church and
cause of Christ while living, that we may share with the sainted dead,
the heaven he promised!

"I must be indulged a word in reference to the entire Cemetery
around us, since already some of you have a special interest in it beyond this enclosure, and as I value it, beyond all price, as another

VISTA HILL.   71

proof of our advancing civilization as a people, and as a most wisely
selected and beautifully disposed burial-place for the dead, for our own
and our sister city.   It is a word of hope, that these lovely grounds
may henceforth, throughout their whole extent, wear only those adorn-
ments which befit or express the Christian's faith.   I regret that any
heathen emblems—emblems rather of a religion of doubt or despair,
than of one which inspires a well-grounded trust, a joyous expectation,
—should ever have been blazoned on its monuments and headstones.*
The inverted torch, the broken column, no more become the cemeteries
of a Christian people, than some of the sad inscriptions in the famous
Père la Chaise, which travellers read there :—'A husband inconsola-
ble'—'A disconsolate wife'—'Broken-hearted parents :' the appropriate
language of hopeless grief alone !   I would have words full of hope,
and confiding faith, and cloudless trust, and filial submission, and a
serene, cheerful piety.   I do not so much object to the obelisk, Egyptian though it be, and savoring, as some think, of an idolatrous homage
of the sun; because its tall shaft, with its pyramidical apex, losing
itself in the air, and pointing to the sky, may seem to speak to the
living of the heavenly home which their departed friends have entered.
But I prefer the cross, the symbol of Christ's victory over death and
the grave.   I prefer the words of Holy Scripture, which speak of 'the
resurrection and the life.'   So that, as we wander here to meditate and
commune with the righteous dead, heaven itself shall seem nearer—the

---

* I fear the above remarks may be misconstrued, or give unnecessary pain to some who have
erected such monuments as are alluded to.   Nothing was farther from my intention.   *As works
of art* only, do I feel that they are open to criticism.   It is not they who paid for them, who are
censured.   Unhappily it is too frequently the case, that he who furnishes the design, seeks only
to meet *the eye* of the employer, and there is too little consideration with both parties, as to the
significance of the emblems chosen.

terrors of the last hour be scattered—the loved who have been taken, come back to our remembrance in all their spiritual beauty,—and our souls, chastened and sobered, be the better prepared for what remains of life's duties, and its last hour."

The Rev. JOHN PIERPONT assisted in these exercises; and the following words from his pen,—to which we are indebted for many Christian lyrics of unsurpassed excellence,—were sung by the assembly, and most appropriately closed the scene:—

> "O God! beneath this Green-Wood shade,—
>   Beneath this blue, autumnal sky,
> Would we, by those we love, be laid,
>   Whene'er it is our time to die.
>
> "The glory of this woodland scene,—
>   These leaves, that came at summer's call, —
> These leaves, so lately young and green,
>   Even now begin to fade and fall.
>
> "So shall we fade and fall at length:
>   Youth's blooming cheek—the silvery hair
> Of reverend age—and manhood's strength,
>   Shall here repose;—Then hear our prayer,
>
> "O Thou, who by thy Son hast said,—
>   From fear of death to set us free,—
> 'God is the God, not of the dead,'
>   That we, for aye, may live in Thee!"

OCEAN HILL.

"They have not perished,—no!
Kind words—remember'd voices, once so sweet—
Smiles radiant long ago—
And features, the great soul's apparent seat,—
All shall come back; each tie
Of pure affection shall be knit again."

WE have in this view an obelisk of considerable height, and in some respects peculiar. The shaft is surrounded by several narrow fillets slightly raised, and connected with other ornaments. Just above the base, on the front side, is a female bust in high relief. A tablet below records the name, virtues, and premature decease of a young wife and mother. The material is brown stone, and the work is finely executed.

Hard by, and just seen through the foliage, is a laborer's cottage. Two of these structures, unlike in form, but both highly picturesque, already adorn the grounds. Others will from time to time be added, until, like a cordon of sentinels, they will surround the Cemetery, enhancing at the same time its security and its beauty.

In happy unison with the immediate scene, and with the thoughts it naturally suggests, mark through the leafy openings those unpretending churches at Flatbush! As seen from this solemn high-place, a sort of Sabbath stillness seems to rest on and around them; while themselves may be deemed fit emblems of the piety and peace they were reared to promote. Still farther to expand and fill the soul, behold where, in the dim, blue distance, stretches far away the mighty sea,—

———— " boundless, endless, and sublime—
The image of Eternity!"

At a short distance from the spot which has just passed under our notice, lie the remains of the Rev. DAVID ABEEL, and a monument will soon rise above them. A brief commemoratory notice in these pages, of this distinguished missionary and most exemplary man, will not, it is believed, be unacceptable.

David Abeel was born in New Brunswick, N. J., A. D. 1804. His father served as an officer in the American navy during the war of the Revolution. The Rev. Dr. Abeel, for many years a distinguished clergyman of the Dutch Collegiate churches in the city of New York, was his uncle. The subject of this sketch was distinguished, even in youth, by unflinching firmness of purpose and action. He early became a keen sportsman, and found health and strength in the exciting toil. The medical profession was his first choice; and he had already made some progress in the study, when new views of life and duty induced him to change his contemplated pursuit, for what he deemed a higher sphere of benevolent action. He entered at once upon the study of divinity, in the Theological School of his church at New Brunswick, and in due time completed the required course, with a reputation for learning and piety, which gave promise of high usefulness.

He was soon settled as pastor of the Dutch Church, just then formed in Athens, N. Y. Here he devoted himself so assiduously to his duties, that a year had not elapsed before his health gave way under the combined exhaustion of excitement and fatigue. To recruit his failing powers, and still serve the cause to which he had consecrated them, he accepted a proposal to minister, during the winter, to a church of his own persuasion in the island of St. Thomas. He returned to the United States; but no entreaties could induce him again to accept a permanent station at home. The miserable degradation and spiritual wants of the heathen world had filled his imagination, and more than touched his heart. Especially had his sympathies long turned towards that mighty empire on the other side of the globe, whose teeming provinces contain one-third part of the human race.

He went first to Canton, in the capacity of chaplain to the numerous seamen who congregate at that port. Soon after he became a regular missionary, under appointment of the board of commissioners for foreign missions, and was stationed at Bankok, in Siam. An enervating climate, and his own toilsome life, soon compelled him to quit his post. After several short voyages for his health, he returned to China, and settled at Macao. But his difficulties returned. He again tried voyaging in the Indian Archipelago. But this had ceased to afford relief; and he reluctantly consented to set out for home. He returned by the way of England. Though so feeble when he sailed, as to be conveyed on a couch to the ship, the passage across the Atlantic proved highly beneficial.

With improving health, his zeal and activity returned. He traversed the land, a missionary apostle, communicating to multitudes some portion of his own earnest benevolence. After a year thus usefully employed, he resolved, in despite of all remonstrance, to return to China. He arrived at Macao previous to the commencement of hos-

tilities on the part of England. He was there during the continuance
of that extraordinary war, and was ready, at its close, to avail himself
of the strange and new position in which it placed the affairs of China.
By a succession of events equally rapid and unexpected, he saw pros-
trated to the ground, the barriers which custom and prejudice had so
long maintained around that singular people. Whatever might be
thought of the motive and principles which led to this result, or of the
means by which it was effected, there seemed no reason to doubt that
it would be mutually beneficial to China and the world. To the
Christian philanthropist especially, whose heart had long bled for so
many millions, "perishing for lack of vision," the event must have
seemed a most auspicious providence. To none could the occurrence
have been more welcome than to the devoted Abeel. For years he
had been laboring almost single-handed. An exhausting climate—im-
paired health—the acquisition of a difficult language—and more than
all, the proverbial exclusiveness of the Chinese, were obstacles sufficient to cool aught but that fervid zeal and love, which the Christian's
faith can alone inspire.

He could now write and speak the language. His prudence, his
conciliatory address and most exemplary character, had given him high
consideration with many of the natives;—and now, at length, the
cannon of the Ocean Queen had been made instrumental in levelling
what seemed the last, great barrier to missionary enterprise. He stationed himself at Amoy, with the intent of entering in earnest on the
great work for which he had so long been preparing. But it was not
so to be. He, who needs not our service, and who often teaches man
a lesson of humility and dependence, as well as of faith and duty, by
removing the most efficient human instruments, saw fit again to reduce

him to extreme weakness. Again he was put on board ship, bound for America, but with no expectation, on the part of his friends, that he would ever reach her shore. He did, however, survive the voyage.

But little more remains to be told. With a characteristic energy of will, which seemed to triumph over physical debility, he visited different and distant parts of the United States. The warmest welcome, the kindest attentions, everywhere awaited this meek and worn-out soldier of the cross. But change of climate, travel, medical skill, and assiduous care, were alike powerless to arrest the progress of disease. A nervous irritability, more difficult, perhaps, than even pain to bear, was his constant attendant. Yet no disturbance of the material organization ruffled his ever even temper, or marred the beauty of his Christian graces. His last days were spent at the house of his friend, Mr. Van Rensselaer, of Albany; and there, on the 6th September, 1846, he quietly expired.

> " Serene, serene,
> He press'd the crumbling verge of this terrestrial scene ;
> Breathed soft, in childlike trust,
> The parting groan ;
> Gave back to dust its dust—
> To heaven its own."

It could have been no common-place character, no ordinary virtues of mind and heart, which won for the subject of our memoir, an esteem so general and enduring. Intellectually, he was clear and discriminating, with great readiness and appropriateness of thought. Resolute of purpose, and energetic in act, he could accomplish a large amount of labor. He was a man of unvarying prudence, and the most considerate kindness. The sincerity and warmth of his good-will, written on his face, imbodied in words of affectionate earnestness, and breathed in tones of the gentlest persuasion, possessed a logic and eloquence that seldom failed to reach the heart. He was distinguished, not so much by any one outshining quality, as by the balanced harmony of all his powers. His was that excellent and rare gift of Heaven, *good sense*. All the sweet urbanities of life he knew and practised; and the high virtues of the Christian missionary, certainly lose none of their lustre, by being associated, as in his case, with those of the gentleman and scholar.

It must be manifest, that a character and life such as we have depicted, could have been inspired and sustained only by a deep-seated and healthy piety. It was this which nerved a sensitive invalid to those circumnavigations of charity,—which sustained him under the depressing fervors of a tropical sun,—which encouraged him along the toilsome task of learning the language,—and which, when friends, and physicians, and fainting nature herself, counselled retirement and repose, carried him again and again from the bed to the field. And what but this, amid the disappointment of long-cherished hopes, and wearisome infirmities of the flesh, could impart that meek resignation and cheerful trust, which made his last hours a scene of perfect peace?

To human view a death like this seems, at first thought, disastrous and premature. It is, however, only the close of a life which should be measured by its intensity, rather than duration. And if,

> " To live in hearts we leave behind,
> Is *not* to die,"

then Abeel still lives;—lives in those words of his which yet survive in memory;—lives in his great example of self-denial and love,—in the very mound that swells above his ashes,—and in each memorial that bears his name.

BATTLE HILL.

"Once this soft turf, this rivulet's sands,
    Were trampled by a hurrying crowd,
And fiery hearts and arméd hands,
    Encounter'd in the battle-cloud.

"Ah! never shall the land forget,
    How gush'd the life-blood of her brave,—
Gush'd, warm with hope and courage yet,
    Upon the soil they fought to save."

INDEPENDENTLY of their present and prospective claims to regard, Green-Wood and its vicinage must ever possess a strong interest, derived from the past. In that vicinity,—upon ground traversed in part by every visiter to the Cemetery, and lying immediately below and around it,—occurred the first serious conflict between the British and American troops, on the memorable 26th of August, 1776. There is indeed reason to believe, that the very spot presented in the plate, was stained that day with patriot blood. It seems strange that the events of that occasion, and the localities of those events, have commanded so little attention. In general, our countrymen have shown any thing but indifference to the spots which were hallowed by the struggles and blood of their fathers. There was scarcely a petty skirmish in New England, which has not had its historian. Every rood of ground trod by hostile feet, has been traced and identified. Upon anniversary returns, thousands have assembled to collect the scattered bones of the glorious dead,—to hear their eulogy from eloquent lips,—and to rear some enduring monument, that shall transmit their names and deeds. What battle, since that of Marathon, has ever concentred upon one small spot of earth, an interest like that which, for seventy years, has clung round Bunker Hill! How have the historian and the novelist, the painter and the architect, the poet and the orator, conspired to enhance its glory! How many millions have visited the spot, to see with their own eyes that "sepulchre of mighty dead," and to press with their own feet, the sod which was wet with Warren's gore!

In contrast with all this, what a story of neglect is that of the battle-ground in Brooklyn! How few of the vast population in its vicinity, know or care aught about it! How very few could even designate the fields where Sullivan and Prescott, until overpowered by an enemy in their rear, fought, with their raw levies, the veterans of Europe, not less bravely than did Prescott at Charlestown, or Stark at Bennington!

Important differences, it is true, distinguish the cases. The engagement at Brooklyn, like that of Bunker Hill, was a defeat—but not, like that, more glorious than most victories. Instead of inspiriting the defenders of freedom, its consequences were depressing and disastrous; and the day was long thought of, as one of mistakes, if not of disgrace. The ground itself came at once into the possession of the British, and so continued to the end of the war. The standard of general intelligence on the island, was neither then, nor for a good while thereafter, very high, while that of patriotism was decidedly low. The popular enthusiasm, so ardent elsewhere, was here unfelt, or for so long a time repressed, that silence and indifference in regard to the matters in question became habitual, and have never been disturbed. Such, it is

BATTLE HILL. 81

believed, are some of the causes of a neglect which is more easily ac-
counted for than justified.

It is due to the brave combatants of that day, that their names and
deeds should be remembered and commemorated, in common with
many others—more distinguished, only because they were more fortu-
nate. To this end we contribute our mite. We would induce some
of the countless visiters of Green-Wood to turn aside, and stand upon
the spot where their fathers once stood, "shoulder to shoulder in the
strife for their country." At least we would have them know, as they
ride along, that the very earth beneath them was reddened in the conflict, which secured to them their great and fair inheritance.

The unsparing hand of improvement is fast sweeping away, not
only the vestiges of all the old defences, but the very hills on which
they were raised, at such expense of treasure and toil. Even the more
distant grounds, beyond the lines of circumvallation, upon which the
fight occurred, have in some instances been materially changed.
The actors in those scenes are all gone. Of traditionary information but little can now be gleaned, and that little will soon have
perished.

That the British would make an early and vigorous effort to obtain
possession of the waters and city of New York, was anticipated, almost
at the commencement of the struggle. The difficulty of defending it
against a powerful army and fleet, which resulted from its position, was
not diminished by the well-known disaffection to the revolutionary
cause, that existed among the inhabitants. But the object was regarded
as of pre-eminent importance. The magnitude of the city itself,—its
convenient and accessible waters,—and particularly its position of command, at one extremity of the great communicating line between the

11

Atlantic and Canada,—were deemed reasons sufficient for maintaining the place at almost any hazard.

As early as February, 1776, General Lee was ordered, with a small force, to New York, to guard against apprehended danger from Sir Henry Clinton and the tories. Defensive works were begun under his direction, and continued to be prosecuted by Lord Stirling and others, until the arrival of Washington in April. For four months more, the work of fortifying went on under his eye, and the most strenuous efforts were made to provide a sufficient defence against the expected attack. At the end of June the British fleet and army began to arrive, and took immediate possession of Staten Island. By the first of August, a powerful fleet and thirty thousand men were stationed on and around it. It was this strong naval and land armament which the American general was expected to oppose and repel. The advantage seemed to be greatly on the side of the enemy. An army mostly of militia-men, who had seen no service, and knew little of discipline,—poorly clothed and ill paid,—with few of the comforts, or even necessaries of the camp,—scantily provided with the arms and munitions which such a service requires, and unsupported by a single war-ship,—were to make good their ground against numbers greatly superior,—accustomed to all the duties of the drill and the field,—and completely furnished with the whole materiel of war.

Being in total uncertainty as to the point of attack, the American commander was compelled to scatter his forces, and to man a great extent of lines. In addition to the defences on Governor's Island, and on both sides of the island of New York, extending up the Hudson and East rivers for many miles, it was thought necessary to guard the western shore of Long Island, where it approaches and commands the city. A series of strong intrenchments stretched from Red Hook quite across to the Wallabout. The woody ridge which extends along nearly the whole eastern side of Brooklyn, was guarded by detachments and pickets posted at all the openings.

Such was the position of affairs when, on the 22d of August, the British commenced landing their troops at New Utrecht, near the spot where Fort Hamilton now stands. Four days afterward, their centre, composed of Hessians, under De Hiester, was at Flatbush; the right wing, commanded by Lords Cornwallis and Percy, extended towards Flatlands; while the left wing, under General Grant, rested on the coast. From the American camp the British centre was four miles, and each of the wings about six miles distant. Very early in the morning of the 27th, two brigades under General Grant, advancing, partly along the coast-road, and partly by Martensis' Lane, which now forms the southern boundary of Green-wood, drove back the regiment stationed in that neighborhood. Lord Stirling, with two regiments of southern troops, was dispatched to oppose them. The day broke as he came in sight of his foe, whose front, on the Gowanus road, was then a little in advance of the present avenue to the Cemetery. The regiment under Col. Atlee, which was retiring before the advancing column, was immediately stationed on the left of the road, near the point where Eighteenth-street intersects it. The other two regiments were planted farther to the left, on the hill now included between Eighteenth and Twentieth-streets. A company of riflemen was posted; partly on the edge of the wood, and partly along a hedge near the foot of the hill. Some relics of this temporary shelter may still be seen,—

" There, where a few torn shrubs the place disclose."

84 GREEN-WOOD ILLUSTRATED.

Having made his arrangements, and while momently expecting the attack, Lord Stirling thus addressed his men:—" The commander, soldiers, of that advancing column, is Major-general Grant. Not long since, I heard him boast, in parliament, that with five thousand men, he would undertake to march from one end of the continent to the other. He may have," added Lord S., "his five thousand men with him now. We are not so many: but I think we are enough to prevent his advancing farther on his march over the continent, than yonder mill-pond."

The British having brought forward a body of light troops, to within a hundred and fifty yards, opened their fire, which was returned with spirit. After two hours' fighting, the light troops retired to the main body. The contest was continued by cannonade for several hours longer, when the noise of firing in their rear, warned the Americans that an immediate retreat had become necessary.

Unfortunately, a pass on the extreme left of the American lines, had been left without any adequate guard. Secret foes, who knew but too well the ground, had apprized the enemy of this advantage. In the course of the night, the British right wing, making a detour through New Lotts, into the road leading from Jamaica to Bedford, was thus enabled to throw itself between the American detachments and their camp. The troops thus assailed by a fire in front and rear, mostly broke and fled. General Sullivan, with about 400 men, was posted on the heights immediately west of Flatbush. Though attacked by overwhelming forces on both sides, he bravely maintained the conflict for nearly three hours, yielding himself a prisoner only when farther resistance had become utterly futile.

While this calamitous affair was going on in the American right and centre, Lord Cornwallis, with a strong force, was advancing toward Gowanus, and had already secured the causeway and bridge at the Upper Mills, when Lord Stirling, in his retreat, came in sight. His men could get back to the inner lines, only by crossing the marsh, and fording or swimming the creek, at some point below. To protect them in this difficult and dangerous operation, Stirling advanced against Cornwallis with 400 men—ordering all the rest to make their escape as best they could. The conflict of this forlorn hope with the veteran troops of Cornwallis, was exceedingly fierce, and at one time, all but successful. But new and overwhelming reinforcements of the enemy, rendered valor and patriotism alike unavailing. The scene of this struggle is supposed to have been principally in the neighborhood of the ancient Cortelyou house, still standing on the old road to Gowanus, with the date, 1699, in large figures on its gable. Numerous skeletons disinterred in its immediate vicinity—and some of them quite recently —leave little doubt respecting the locality.

Stirling, having by this engagement secured the safety of his main body, made an attempt to escape with his small surviving remnant. But he was now hemmed completely in, and submitting to his fate, he surrendered. Several historians,—and the traditions of the neighborhood, accredited even to this day,—have affirmed that large numbers perished in attempting to cross the marsh. The same statement was made by General Howe, in his official dispatch. It is, nevertheless, undoubtedly a mistake. A letter is extant, written a few weeks after the engagement, by Col. Haslet, who commanded a regiment in Stirling's brigade, and was one of those who crossed the marsh. He states, unequivocally, that the retreat over the marsh "was effected in good order, with the loss of one man drowned in passing."

There is no reason to suppose that there was much fighting within what is now the Cemetery enclosure. But sharpshooters are known to have been perched in and among the trees, which then covered thickly that whole range of hills; and tradition has it, that one small party of riflemen was surrounded and exterminated, on the very eminence presented in the plate. That these practised marksmen would find little mercy at the hands of an enemy, which had experienced the fatal precision of their aim, was only to be expected. In one instance, at least, a British officer, unwilling to remain the object of their too partial attentions, left his post and men, and took shelter in a neighboring farm-house.

As the bodies of the victims in this struggle were mostly interred where they fell, there can be little doubt that Green-wood is the sleeping-place of some of them. It is time that a spot were set apart, on its most commanding and beautiful eminence, in honor of these early martyrs for freedom. Here should be deposited the relics which have been, or from time to time shall be, recovered, in the numerous excavations now going on, within and around these grounds. It may be difficult, nay, impossible to distinguish friend from foe. It matters not. To the sturdy Briton, who in death remembered his dear island-home; —the poor, hired Hessian, whose last thoughts were of his wife and children on the far-distant Rhine;—and the patriot yeoman, whose dying hour was sweetened by the reflection that he fell in a righteous cause;—to each and all, an honorable burial.

"Gather him to his grave again,
And solemnly and softly lay,
Beneath the verdure of the plain,
The warrior's scatter'd bones away."

BATTLE HILL.

And here we may allude to another act of justice and gratitude. which ought not longer to be delayed. It is well known that the remains of the American prisoners, who died in such numbers in the British prison-ships, and whose bodies were huddled into the earth on a hill in North Brooklyn, were a few years since piously rescued from desecration, and consigned to a vault not far from the entrance to the United States Navy Yard. This arrangement—the act of one generous individual—must, of necessity, be regarded as temporary. The spot and structure are destitute not only of security against future molestation, but of the dignity and solidity which become such a tomb. Some faint efforts have indeed been made to accomplish their removal to Green-wood. But why await the tardy action of the General Government? Is there not enough of patriotism and gratitude in these two great and wealthy communities, to raise the means for a decent, nay, for a noble tribute to those unfortunate men, who died for their country as truly, as though they had fallen on the battle-field, and in the very hour of victory? Taken while defending that country's cause, were they less to be commiserated while living, or less to be honored and deplored in death,—that they were compelled to experience the pestilential damps and nauseous horrors of those dismal cabins, into which they were crowded like so many sheep? How many fond husbands and fathers,—how many well-beloved sons, amid those appalling scenes of want, sickness, and death, must have sighed for the comforts and the solace of the homes, which they were never more to see! But we forbear. Our strongest conception of such a scene, how far short must it fall of the stern reality! In that masterpiece of reasoning and eloquence, the Oration for the Crown, the incomparable orator, arguing the point, that well-meant endeavor, and not success, is the test and proof of merit, reminds his countrymen that their funeral honors had ever been paid to all who fell in the service of Athens—the unsuccessful as well as the victorious brave. The citizens of a great and flourishing state, in the brightest era of civilization and Christianity, should learn a lesson here, from pagan Greece. Must some Demosthenes arise, with superhuman power, to explain and enforce their duty, before they will hear and obey its dictates ?

The position assigned to Lord Stirling's troops and General Grant's brigade, in the plans of the battle which accompany Marshall's History, and Sparks' Washington,—a plan which has been lately copied, without correction, in Duer's Life of Stirling,—is very erroneous. On those plans, the contending forces are placed about opposite to Yellow Hook; whereas, in fact, Stirling did not advance beyond the middle of Gowanus Bay—nor farther south than a hill on Wyckoff's grounds, lying between what, in the future topography of the city, will be Eighteenth and Twentieth-streets. There was, however, if we may credit tradition, a little fighting in the neighborhood of Yellow Hook— a slight skirmish, not noticed in any of the published accounts, between the advancing British and Atlee's retiring regiment, in which a few lives were lost.

The Knickerbocker Magazine for April, 1839, contains an interesting article on the battle of Long Island, prepared from a discourse originally delivered before the New York Historical Society, by Samuel Ward, Jr. It is illustrated by an engraved sketch of the battle-ground, which is believed to be, by far, the most accurate of any yet published. The plan was drawn by Major D. B. Douglass, formerly of the U. S. army, from personal inspection. The major, to whose energy and taste Green-wood Cemetery is largely indebted, had

BATTLE HILL.   89

examined the entire battle-ground, with the eye of a soldier as well as surveyor, and the sketch which he furnished, may be relied on as authentic and complete.

Much has been written respecting the causes of this defeat. The sudden illness of General Greene, who had superintended the fortifications, and knew all the circumstances and necessities of the American position,—the neglect, consequent, perhaps, on the change of commanders, to guard properly the Jamaica road,—were doubtless the immediate causes of the surprise, the rout, the capture of two generals, and of so many soldiers.

But had it been otherwise,—had every precaution been taken,—little more could have been done, or was probably expected, than to check the advancing foe. The American forces might have retreated in good order, with comparatively small loss—but they must have retreated. Five thousand raw recruits—few of whom had ever been in battle, and most of whom must have fought without cover—could not long have resisted twenty thousand well-appointed veterans. The real wonder is, that they did so well. It was the first fight of the war, which took place in the open field. To no greater trial of courage could those patriot, but unpractised soldiers have been put. Praise to their memories!—most of them stood well the test. They boldly faced, or repeatedly charged the foe—and fled or yielded, only when longer resistance would have been madness, and utter extermination.

There is, perhaps, no period in the revolutionary struggle, to which we can recur more profitably, than to the anxious summer and the gloomy autumn of 1776. The courage which survived such disasters; the hope which lived on amid so many discouragements; the faith which no reverses nor difficulties could shake, and which finally rose triumphant over them all,—have long commanded, and must ever command the wonder of the world. And shall they not awaken something more than admiration in us, to whose benefit they have inured so largely?

It was while chilled by these blasts of adversity,—while watered, as it were, by the tears of those great spirits, who for a long time could bring to the suffering cause little besides their own indomitable energies,—that the tree of freedom was sending its roots outward and downward, and gathering strength for that rapidly expanding growth, which marked the summer of its prosperity. It is not, be it ever remembered, the magnitude of armies—the masterly tactics by which mighty masses are made to march and countermarch—the brilliancy of the charge—the steady bravery of the repulse—or all the bloody statistics of the most ensanguined conflict, which can attach to military operations a true and lasting interest. A hundred terrible battles gave to Napoleon a fame unequalled in the annals of war, and that "name at which the world grew pale." But they were unconnected with high principle,—they were followed by no great, benignant results,—and in the sober estimate of future times, will rank, in importance, far below those Fabian campaigns which laid the foundations of an empire, that already walks, with its rank unchallenged, among the foremost powers of earth.

Not in vain, then, was even the *defeat* of Brooklyn; not in vain, the anguish with which the usually calm spirit of Washington was that day torn. Not in vain were those two anxious days and nights which he passed on horseback, and which saved from death or captivity, nine thousand men. These, and more,—the reluctant abandonment of the city,—the cowardice and desertion of the militia,—the loss of the forts,

—and that sad retreat of the reduced, discouraged, barefooted, and half-naked army through the Jerseys,—were all needed. In the immortal letters and dispatches of the great commander, and in the painful annals of the time, we read the cost and the value of what we are now enjoying. Without these we had not fully known how inherent, how enduring and elastic is the power of an earnest and virtuous patriotism. Without them, even the transcendent name of Washington could not have filled the mighty measure of its fame.

THE PILOT'S MONUMENT.

" Some, scarcely parted twice a cable's length
From those who on the firm earth safely stand,
Shall madly watch the strain'd, united strength,
And cheers and wavings of the gallant band,
Who launch their life-boat with determined hand.
Ah ! none shall live that zealous aid to thank :
The wild surge whirls the life-boat back to land,—
The hazy distance suddenly grows blank,—
In that last, laboring plunge, the fated vessel sank."

THIS structure commemorates the loss of a brave and humane man.
THOMAS FREEBORN was one of those hardy mariners, whose profes-
sional duty keeps them almost perpetually on the sea, and whose
daring little barks often meet the returning ship, while yet many
leagues from port. He attempted to bring in the ship John Minturn,
in the severe storm of the 14th February, 1846. In spite of every
effort, she was driven upon the Jersey shore,—and Freeborn, with a
large part of the ship's company, was drowned, though close to the
beach, and within hail of hundreds, who unfortunately could afford
them no relief. His brother pilots, with a liberality which does them
great credit, reared this imposing monument. On a sarcophagus,
which rests upon a massive base, is placed a ship's capstan, with a
cable coiled around it. From this rises a mast, whose truncated top
is surmounted by a small and well-executed statue of Hope, supported

by her anchor, and pointing to the skies. The front of the sarcophagus bears, in relief, a ship and a schooner, mutilated by the storm, and tossed by the waves.

Its height and position make the monument a conspicuous object from the bay,—and will often arrest the eye of the pilot as he goes and comes on his hazardous but responsible errands. If it remind him of his own possible fate,—it will assure him also that the faithful discharge of duty is never without its encouragement:

Æternumque locus Palinuri nomen habebit.

This tempest once blew soft and fair,—
This storm-gust seem'd bright, pictured air,—
These torrents, rushing from the sky,
Were dews below, or clouds on high.

The fires, in boreal flames that play'd
So softly o'er last evening's shade,
Now fierce athwart the darkness glare,
Riving, with forked bolts, the air.

These angry waves, that swell and roar,
Late broke in ripples on the shore,—
Or where yon sea-dogs rend their prey,
Calm as a sleeping infant lay.

Swift and secure the sea-boy glides—
But ah! what peril near him hides;
Beneath him, or above him cast
The sunken rock, or furious blast.

Christian! thy PILOT walks the wave,
Full wise to guide—full strong to save;
His faintest word shall still the roar
Of winds, and bear thee safe to shore.

THE GERMAN LOTS—THE ODD-FELLOWS' GROUNDS.

" Pilgrims that journey for a certain time,—
    Weak birds of passage crossing stormy seas,
To reach a better and a brighter clime,—
    We find our parallels and types in these !
    Meanwhile, since death, and sorrow, and disease,
Bid helpless hearts a barren pity feel ;
    Why to the Poor should check'd compassion freeze ?
Brothers, be gentle to that one appeal,—
Want is the only wo God gives you power to heal !"

The enclosures presented in this plate, are upon Lawn Avenue. One of them is a public lot, where a single grave, at moderate cost, can always be had. Another, of about the same size, belongs to several German families. The ardor with which these emigrants cherish all the ties of kin and country, is well known. Far away from the homes and graveyards of their Fatherland, it is natural that they should cling together in life,—and that, in death, they should wish to lie side by side. Beyond the Public Lot extend, for a considerable distance, the grounds of the Odd-Fellows. Several Lodges of this charitable and great fraternity have here made provision for their last resting-place. This spot has already become populous ; and hundreds of long low mounds, in close juxtaposition, betoken the aspect which, through its entire extent, Green-Wood must assume at no distant day.

NAMES OF THE ORIGINAL SUBSCRIBERS

TO THE

RURAL CEMETERIES ILLUSTRATED.

NEW-YORK,
CITY.

Achelis, Thomas
Ackerman, James M.
Adams, J. C.
Agnew, A. M.
Agnew, John T.
Aldis, Charles J.
Aldrich, E. T.
Alford, S. M.
Allaire, Alexander
Allen, Francis
Allen, John
Anderson, Dr. James
Anderson, John Jacob
Anderson, Wm. C.
Anthony, Thomas R.
Archer, Mrs. Daniel O.
Arnold, Dr. Wm.
Arthur, Edward H.
Ashley, Dr. James
Asten, Wm. B.
Atherton, F.
Atterbury, Wm.
Atwater, George M.
Avery, S. P.
Ayres, Dr. Daniel
Ayres, Robert
Bagioli, Mrs. Antonio
Bailey, Joseph
Baker, Miss ——
Baker, P. H.
Baker, Wm.
Baldwin, N. Andrew
Banks, Henry W.
Banks, Wm.
Bannister, James
Baptist, Anthony, Jr.
Barker, Mrs. Abraham
Barker, Mrs. Eliza
Barker, J. O.
Barker, J. Willard
Barker, Dr. Luke
Barritt, Charles F.
Bartow, E. J.
Bartram, Mrs. Thomas
Bass, ——
Bayles, N. H.
Bayley, W. A.
Beale, J. C.
Beardsley, L. T.
Beebe, Wm. J.
Bell, John
Belloni, Louis J.
Benedict, Caleb S.
Benson, Charles S.
Betts, Wm.
Betts, Wm. W.
Bill, Edward
Bird, Clinton G.
Black, Mrs. Mary
Blakeley, Mrs. Andrew
Blatchford, Samuel D.
Blenis, Mrs. O.
Blunt, G. B.
Bogle, James
Bolmore, B

Bonnett, Peter R.
Bookhout, E.
Booth, Samuel
Bottomley, John
Bouton, L. S.
Boyd, John I.
Boyd, Robert H.
Boyle, John C.
Bowman, Samuel
Bradbury, J. K.
Bradish, Mrs. Luther
Bradshaw, H. B.
Brady, Archibald C.
Braisted, Wm. C.
Brandon, Alexander
Brandon, George
Brass, J. D.
Breck, Miss ——
Brennan, G. S.
Brewer, Merwin R.
Briggs, James M.
Briggs, Mrs. John
Brigham, John Tyler
Brind, Henry
Brizee, George M.
Brock, John
Brower, John L.
Brown, Isaac H.
Brown, John C.
Brown, John F.
Brown, J. F.
Brown, Wm. Smith
Brown, Geo. Washington
Bryson, P. M.
Buchanan, R. M.
Buck, Wm. C.
Buckingham, George A.
Buckley, W. F.
Bunker, Mrs. B. F.
Burnap & Babcock
Burrill, Wm. B.
Bushnell, O.
Busteed, Richard
Butler, James R.
Butler, Marcus B.
Butterworth, J. F.
Byrd, George J.
Chase, Nelson
Cumming, J. P.
Conger, A. B.
Clark, Edward P.
Cotrell, B. S.
Cannon, Charles James
Cole, Jacob
Candee, E. W.
Cany, Edward
Cleaveland, J.
Cook, Zebedee
Cartwright, A.
Cutlip, Henry E.
Collins, George
Crane, J. J.
Clarke, T. E.
Cropsey, J. E.
Childs, B. F.
Coe, F. A.
Carter, James C.
Carter, R.

Coddington, Widow Mary
Crolius, Clarkson
Clark, L. E.
Cooke, Thomas W.
Carpenter, Warren
Codman, Wm.
Clark, Wm. Young
Crane, Augustus
Crane, Theodore
Connolly, Charles M.
Clirehugh, Vair
Childs, Wm.
Compton, Mansfield
Churchill, Wm. E.
Comstock, D. A.
Cushing, G. W. B.
Christman, Charles G.
Canfield, Edward
Coles, Francis B.
Carleton, C. G.
Clayton, W. A.
Clayton, James H.
Carroll, Anthony B.
Christianson, Edward T.
Chapin, Dr. John R.
Crocker, Mrs. Eben B.
Cobb, Alexander
Classen, James M.
Cock, Dr. Thomas
Cortelyou, Peter C.
Corwin, John
Chapman, J. G.
Church, Miss Mary
Cornell & Jackson
Campbell, James
Catlin, Mrs. John S.
Carroll, J. B.
Champlin, W. C.
Colvin, Mrs. Andrew J.
Colman, Mrs. Wm.
Cragin, B. F.
Clark, Ebenezer
Cooper, Benson S.
Charles, Maurice
Carpenter, Miss Ann A.
Colgate, Mrs. Sarah
Carlile, Thomas
Carlile, N. D.
Cox, J. F.
Carpenter, Widow Sarah
Chescbrough, E.
Crosley, C. W.
Dodge, Henry S.
Dickinson, J. J.
Dowley, John
Douglas, A. E.
Day, Thomas
De Witt, J. H.
Dole, Nathaniel L.
Dickinson, Edwin S.
Daniel, R.
Dreyer, F. A., Jr.
Dole, Wm.
Duryee, Jacob
Duryee, Mrs. Isaac
Downs, Mrs. Benjamin F.
Dashwood, G. L.
Dunham, Mrs. John B.

Disbrow, Wm. D.
Davis, Samuel C.
Dunkin, Miss Hester
Dean, Miss Louisa
Dunham, John
Dunlap & Thompson
Dougherty, Mrs. Jos'ne T.
Dayton, James S.
Day, Charles J.
Davie, Miss Margaret S.
Dodge, Wm.
De Coppett, Edward
Dolby, Mrs. Wm.
Durand, A. B.
Dwight, Edmund
Duryee, Mrs. Abraham
Davis, Wm. J.
Dill, Vincent
Donohue, James
Edwards, Jonathan
Ellis, R. O.
Edwards, Alfred
Earnest, James
Eggert, John
Elliott, John M.
Earle, Edward S.
Edsall, James
Evans, James
Erben, Peter
Elliott, Dr. Samuel M.
Eagleson, E.
Erving, Washington
Erving, Wm.
Edson, Clement M.
Elliott, Alfred
Field, Wm.
Franklin, Morris
Frost, Samuel
Francis, L.
Fox, Samuel M.
Field, Cyrus W.
Flanders, Benjamin
Follett, R. F.
Finn, A. T.
Fitzgerald, Ezekiel
Freeman, Charles P.
Fletcher, Oscar B.
Freeman, Dr. A.
Fowler, S. P.
Fairfield, Mrs. S. L.
Finch, Nathaniel
Foster, James
Flanelly, Mrs. Michael
Farless, Miss ——
Floyd, Mrs. Auguste
Forsyth, John
Ferris, John H.
Farre, J. R.
Fiske, E. W.
French, Daniel
Force, John C.
Gifford, George
Griffith, G. W.
Gunther, Christian G.
Gerding, G. F.
Griffin, John F.
Gimbrede, G. N.
Gibson, Lewis

Goodhue, Jonathan
Griffin, James
Gage, Wm.
Gill, John
Green, Mrs. Joseph
Giles, John S.
Goss, Mrs. Frances M.
Goldsmith, Dr. Alban
Geissenhainer, F. W., Jr
Gage, Miss S. E.
Giffin, Francis
Garner, T.
Green, Dr. Horace
Greenwood, Isaac l.
Grinnell, Mrs. H.
Gray, John A.
Griffin, Francis
Gage, H. Nelson
Gillespie, G. D. H.
Halliday, Thomas A.
Hunt, S. B.
Howe, H. A.
Hopkins, W. A
Hopkins, W. A., Jr.
Hoffman, S. B., Jr.
Hammond, Samuel
Holmes, J. E.
Hoyt, C.
Hincken, W. W.
Hoffman, Martin
Haviland, R. F.
Harris, J. D.
Harris, Thomas B.
Hanna, John
Hyer, Samuel D.
Hague, John
Herring, F. W
Hayes, H. N.
Hubbard, Samuel N.
Hubbard, Wm. H.
Howard, John T.
Hart, Lucius
Hoadley, David
Hunt, Samuel V.
Hart, Francis
Henrique, Charles
Hills, Jarvis H
Hill, Henry S.
Harmon, J.
Hoffman, A. W.
Hoyt, J. K.
Hoyt, Seymour
Howe, Augustus
Henderson, Alexander, Jr
Hunt, Thomas
Hardorp, J.
Hoeber, W. A.
Haggerty, Ogden
Hastie, W. S.
Hoe, Peter S.
Hawk, Miss Mary
Haviland, Stephen A.
Hatfield, Amos F.
Harbeck, John H.
Horton, R.
Haywood, G. M
Holbrook, E.
Hall, Mrs. A. D

NAMES OF THE ORIGINAL SUBSCRIBERS.

Hone, Philip	Krebs, Rev. John M.	Mott, Dr. Valentine	Pentz, B.	Siffken, Francis E.
Hanghwout, E. V.	Koop, G. H.	Mowbray, Wesley	Protheroe, Robert	St. Felix, George Edward
Heather, Wm.	Kenward, Thomas	Miller, Mrs. George C.	Prentice, J. H.	Sand, C. H.
Hutchins, George H.	Kimball, Mrs. M. T. C.	Malcolm, J. F.	Packer, Wm. S.	Schröder, H.
Heard, James, Jr.	Kee, O.	Mitchell, Mrs. Catharine	Putnam, O. C.	Sherman, Byron
Haynel, Dr. A.	Livingston, Crawford	Marshall, Mrs. Wm. H.	Puffer, George S.	Schufeldt, W. T.
Hubbard, N. T.	Lent, Mortimer	Miller, Mrs. Mary	Petrie, Miss J. A.	Simpson, Frederick
Hutton, Rev. Dr. M. S.	Lyman, John H.	Maybie, Abraham P.	Polhamus, John	Smith, James T.
Hoyt, J.	Lyman, Lewis	Mason, Rev. Cyrus	Phelps, George	Southwick, Nathan
Hurlbut, Mrs. H. A.	Livingston, A.	Mather, Miss	Purdy, Mrs. Wm. T.	Slote, Henry L.
Hart, Mrs. R. H.	Lasak, Francis W.	Mortimer, G. T.	Parsons, Mrs. ——	Silleck, Daniel C.
Hinshelwood, Robert	Langley, W. C.	Milnor, Charles E.	Perry, Mrs. Frances S.	Sadlier, Dennis
Hall, Henry P.	Lewis, Ezra	Mace, John	Platt, John	Smith, Andrew A.
Hopkins, Mrs. ——	Lethbridge, Robert	Mann, Wm.	Post, Mrs. Lavinia	Säs, A. Wm.
Heroy, J. M.	Lord, S.	Mitchell, Miss Mary	Phyfe, J. M.	Southwick, G. W.
Halsey, Mrs. Elmor C.	Leland, J. A.	Meeks, Mrs. Sarah C.	Platt, Nathaniel C.	Steel, Joseph
Hamilton, Jacob	Leeds, Samuel, Jr.	Morrison, Mrs. John C.	Parish, Henry	Smith, Hiram
Harris, Dennis	Locke, John D.	Martin, Mrs. Wm.	Pierce, Mrs. Edward	Smith, Stephen
Hudson, Miss Bridget M.	Lewis, W. H.	Martin, Isaac	Pell, Wm. W.	Sandford, Charles B.
Hall, Geo. L.	Linen, James	Moffat, Miss Mary	Pritchard, Mrs. A.	Schultz, Mrs. J. S.
Hanks, Owen G.	Lawrence, D. Lysack	Marsh, Mrs. Willet P.	Pope, J. L.	Sands, A. B.
Haviland, Walter	Little, Edward	Mathews, J. Seymour	Prosser, Thomas	Shepherd, Thomas S.
Hill, James R.	Lord, Joseph N.	Meakim, Alexander	Pomeroy, B., Jr.	Stebbins, Russell
Hadden, David	Libby, Ira	Mac Gregor, Daniel	Quintarel, O. P.	Scofield, Mrs. W. H.
Hoffman, Mrs. L. M.	Lord, C. H.	McCormick, R.	Ray, Robert	Seymour, W. M.
Hewett, Mrs. Thomas	Lothian, George B.	McLean, J.	Richardson, G.	Stilwell, James
Horn, A. F. M.	Lloyd, James O.	McKesson, John W.	Ridgway, Charles	Seeley, Richard
Holden, H.	Lang, John	McCurdy, R. H.	Rose, Wm. M.	Sitcher, Mrs. Andrew
Hall, Charles	Lowe, B.	McEvers, Bache	Roe, G. Scott	Sweet, Ezra B.
Hampton, Alonzo R.	Lester, Andrew	McNeil, J	Rice, W. W.	Smith, Miss Elizabeth
Hull, J. C.	Lewis, John Walker	McBride, Henry	Rothmaler, B.	Stone, Samuel B.
Hartshorne, Miss C. C.	Ludlam, Miss Eliza	Mc Lean, Henry	Rossiter, C. D., Jr.	Soulard, B.
Health, Mrs. Francis	Lewis, Benedict, Jr.	McNulty, Marvin	Ritchie, Charles	Schermerhorn, A.
Handlin, Wm.	Lowrie, Rev. John C.	McLaughlin, G. P.	Ross, Andrew	Stout, Theodore
Hassal, John S.	Lane, Smith E.	McGrath, M.	Robinson, B. F.	Schmidt, Mrs. John W.
Haight, Mrs. Charles	Leroy, Jacob	McChesney, Wm. F.	Randall, David	Sattathwaite, J. B.
Hill, James A.	Lane, Miss C. A.	McKnight, Dr. Scott	Root, Russell C.	Sandford, Marcus B.
Ives, David S.	Lehman, C. H.	McGown, John R.	Rowland, George	Seeley, W. A.
Ironsides, Robert B.	Lockwood, J. B.	McCoon, Mrs. Mary	Read, Geo. W.	Swan, John
Ingersoll, C. L.	Lewis, George	McLeay, Thomas W.	Richards, W. W.	Smith, Thomas W.
Jones, S. T.	Leroy, Peter V.	McKee, J. W.	Rozat, Guillaume	Stuart, R. L.
Jenkins, H. B.	Lawrence, Luther M.	Newbold, George	Raper, B. W.	Smith, Jotham
Johnson, Henry W.	Lossing, Benson J.	Nelson, George P.	Richards, Thomas F.	Schuchardt, C. W. F.
Johnson, Theodore	Larue, Isaac	Noyes, Samuel	Robinson, James P.	Squire, Charles
Jones, E.	Lawrence, Wm. S.	Naylor, Joseph	Rockwell, Samuel D.	Sears, Robert
Johnson, Henry	Mottram, M.	Niles, George W.	Root, Albert	Storm, Isaac A.
Jordan, Conrad	Morewood, J. R.	Noble, John Sanford	Relyea, Mrs. Peter	Seymour, Isaac N.
Johnson, Miss C. J.	Mills, J. W.	Nivens, Miss Mary F.	Rowell, Charles S.	Seaver, Benjamin F.
Jaques, J. C.	Miller, John H.	Nolton, Mrs. R. H.	Robson, Dr. Benjamin R.	Strong, Edward
Jones, W.	Marvin, R.	Noe, M.	Redway, Miss S.	Searl, Lewis F.
Jackson, J. A.	Meserole, Jacob	Newell, Wm. E.	Reed, John	Speidel, Mrs. C. M.
Jenkins, Thomas W.	Morrison, Alexander	Nicholl, Mrs. Samuel	Rich, Abraham B.	Schmidt, Dr. John W., Jr.
Johnson, Miss Sarah	Morrison, James	Ogden, Richard H.	Rankin, Wm.	Sickels, W. B.
Johnson, W. S.	Matthews, J. M.	Okell, Wm.	Ridabock, Mrs. M. A.	Stoneall, J. C.
Jackson, Augustus	Marvin, A. B.	Oakley, Richard	Richardson, Mrs. S.	Senior, Edward H.
Johnson, Mrs. Charles E.	Mead, Ralph	Ormsbee, J. H., Jr.	Reed, Mrs. Sarah	Thompson, Jonathan, Jr.
Jackson, Mrs. Abram W.	Macy, F. H.	Otten, Hinrich	Rapetti, Mrs. Michele	Thomas, L. W
Jones, Mrs. Susan	Mead, J. S.	Otis, Wm. H.	Ralph, Dr. Joseph	Thorn, J. M.
Jacobus, David	Messellier, H. L.	Ovington, W. H.	Selden, Dudley	Taggard, Wm.
Kemble, Wm.	Marvin, A. S.	Oakley, J. W.	Stiles, Samuel	Treadwell, W. E.
Kingsland, Miss H. C.	Mead, Walter	Osborn, Abner	Smith, James F.	Tomes, Francis
Kinsman, Israel	Morrison, David	Osborn, Mrs. Wm.	Smith, Algernon Sidney	Titus, S. R.
Kobbe, Wm.	Martin, R., Jr.	Oakley, R. S.	Smillie, W. C.	Thorburn, James, Jr.
Kimball, D. S.	Marsh, Wm. R.	Orr, John W.	Smith, Augustus N.	Talman, W. H.
Kissam, A.	Moore, J. T.	O'Boyce, Miss Phœbe	Sluyter, James S.	Tompkins, E. O.
Kearney, J. R.	Munson, Robert	Priest, Wm. H.	Stevens, W. H.	Thomas, John
Kissam, Wm. A.	Mercantile Library Assoc'n	Peck, George B.	Stebbins, H. G.	Timpson, J. H.
Kellogg, W. C.	Mangain, Daniel	Phalen, James	Strong, Geo. W.	Townsend, John L.
King, James L.	Mullany, E. B.	Prime, E.	Stout, A. G.	Townsend, Wm. H.
Ketcham, J.	Macy, Miss Elizabeth	Phillips, Louis	Smith, Jesse C.	Thorne, R. J.
King, John	Macy, Miss Martha	Powell, E. S.	Spear, George	Taylor, Gordon P.
Knapp, S. K.	Mead, S. M.	Polley, Grahams	Skippon, Robert	Trimble, D.
Kneeland, Furman L.	Miles, W. B.	Platt, G. W.	Scrymser, J.	Tillou, Charles D.
Knock, Thomas	Miles, A.	Proctor, G. W.	Schobel, James	Thall, John F.
King, Wm. M.	Merriam, W. B.	Paret, John	Seaman, J. A.	Turnure, John L.
Kissam, S.	Matthews, J.	Perry, R. B.	Shaw, James M.	Thompson, Andrew
Kingsland, D.	Marsh, J. P.	Polhemus, Theodore	Smith, Charles H.	Taber, C. C.
Knapp, Stephen H.	Mumford, J. Paige	Peck, Alfred P.	Smalley, Geo. C.	Tompson, Mrs. Thomas
Kingsley, E. M.	Moore, Nathaniel F.	Poole, Wm.	Smith, Thomas U.	Tinson, T. R.
Key, F. C.		Phelps, G. W.	Strong, Damas	Taylor, H. S.

NAMES OF THE ORIGINAL SUBSCRIBERS.

Traphagan, Mrs. C.
Taylor, J. D.
Turner, John
Tucker, Mrs. Joseph
Tallman, Mrs. George D.
Teale, John P.
Trenor, Dr. James
Taylor, Mrs. John
Tobitt, Mrs. John H.
Thompson, H. G.
Tuffs, Lucien
Turnure, Abraham
Totten, Mrs. J. M.
Underhill, Daniel
Unkart, E.
Van Santvoord, Cornelius
Vandervoort, P. H.
Van Nest, Henry
Varick, James L.
Van Rensselaer, H. R.
Valentine, A. A.
Vyse, Charles
Valentine, Richard C.
Vanderbeck, James
Van Horn, John
Vincent, Benjamin
Van Saun, Mrs. John A.
Van Raden, Benjamin
Vandervoort, David
Van Wagenen, G.
Van Antwerp, Mrs. James
Varick, Dr. T. R.
Vallance, Mrs. C.
Van Blarcom, Mrs. A.
Vermilye, J. D.
Van Der Werken, Mrs.
Weed, Nathaniel
Wright, C. W.
Winslow, James
Whitney, Stephen
Watkins, C. L.
Wakeman, Wm.
Webb, Charles D.
Willets, Daniel T.
Wilmot, J.
Waldron, J. P.
Wallace, John
Whitlock, Mrs. T. E
Ward, Miss
Woram, John
Wheeler, Jackson
Ward, James
West, Mrs. Joseph I.
Wilson, Mrs. Nathaniel
Whitney, Benjamin S.
Webb, Mrs. Wm.
Walker, J. N.
Woodruff, David
Wilson, Mrs. B. M.
Wood, Mrs. E. B.
Westervelt, Daniel
White, N.
Williams, E. P.
Whittemore, Mrs. S.
Walsh, Braine
Wyman, L. B.
Williams, Mrs. Elizabeth
Whittemore, Wm. T.
Winser, John R.
Watson, Mrs. E. Baker
Washburn, H. A
Weed, Wm. C.
White, F.
White, Edward
White, R. H.
Wells, Joseph C
Webb, G.
Weeks, E. A.
Wenman, J. F.
Warrin, John

White, R. Cornell
Ward, B.
Wood, George W.
White, John T.
Waterbury, H. H.
Wells, Charles
Wood, R. E.
Walsh, George
Walsh, W. W.
Wiley, John
Wyman, R. A.
Warford, W. K.
White, W. A.
Webster, George C.
White, E.
Watmough, R. B.
Whiting, W. E.
Waller, Alfred
Wright, E.
Wesson, David
Wesson, Andrew
Wilcomb, J.
Wood, George S.
Winter, J. W.
Youle, John C. B.
Young, John
Young, Stephen B.
Zimmermann, John C.

———

BROOKLYN, N. Y.

Adams, Mrs. B.
Abraham, George
Arcularius, P. J.
Atlantic Lodge, No. 50, } I. O. of O. F. {
Atkins, David S.
Ames, —
Atkins, J.
Adams, P.
Bowne, Samuel
Brooks, T.
Bennett, Winant J.
Bullock, M.
Buck, Mrs. ——
Bradford, W.
Briggs, Mrs. J.
Blackburne, R. C.
Butler, James G.
Bond, Miss
Bennam, John
Bellingham, Dr. J.
Buck, Thomas W.
Bailey, Robert
Banks, M. E.
Brush, J. B.
Boyd, Miss
Barney, Hiram
Bryant, E. W.
Beman, W.
Barter, John
Ballard, L.
Beam, Gilbert
Bridge, E.
Beam, Mrs.
Berry, John
Blanch, John
Bergen, Peter
Burbank, Mrs. Wm.
Burrill, George
Bergen, Garrett G.
Bergen, John
Bennett, Mrs. Remsen
Baldwin, B.
Brower, Samuel
Bates, J. A.
Ball, Mrs. Mary

Bicknell, Miss Henrietta
Booth, Mrs. R.
Bigelow, Louisa
Barkuloo, Miss M. A.
Burkuloo, Tunis
Burtis, O. D.
Christianson, Nicholas
Coope, David
Cox, Henry
Conklin, Solomon
Childs, G. C.
Conklin, H. N.
Campbell, Alexander
Cartwright, W.
Copland, J. M.
Cortelyou, John
Cullen, Dr. H. J.
Craven, Tunis
Chapman, W. P.
Cornell, Chauncey
Cowing, James A.
Clark, H. L.
Cook, Francis
Cross, J. A.
Collier, Mrs. Mary
Dwight, Miss Caroline E.
Deane, Mrs. Maria
Dyckman, F. H.
Davis, Mrs. Margaret
Davis, B. W.
Demming, Miss
Dodge, Mrs.
Duryee, Jacob
Day, Willard
Decker, Dr. D.
Demott, Peter
De Cost, ——
De Le Ree, Miss
Dent, Thomas
Edey, Henry
Eames, ——
Ellison, Sarah
Eberle, Mrs. Matilda
Evans, Wm.
Eskildson, Mrs. Mary
Elwell, J. W.
Eagle Lodge, No. 94, } I. O. of O. F. {
Evans, Ira P.
Field, Charles A.
Farley, Frederick A.
Fletcher, H. R.
Fobes, Mrs. A.
Graves, R.
Gracie, Mrs.
Galt, George
Gardner, Miss Jane E.
Garrison, J.
Graham, J. B.
Gilfilland, Dr. George
Graham, Augustus
Greenwood, J.
Greene, Mrs. Sidney
Greene, R. H.
Guy, Samuel S.
Gansevoort, Mrs. S. H.
Gratacap, J. L.
Granger, James
Gilbert, Joseph
Giffin, Abraham
Grove, G.
Garrison, Dr. Nelson A.
Herbert, Sidney C.
Hall, John
Hall, George
Harvey, C. A.
Holt, Mrs. J. P.
Hartmann, W.
Humphrey, Mrs. James
Harrison, Miss Mary

Hurd, Dr. T. W.
Hyde, Dr. Lucius
Harper, Mrs. J. W.
Hutchins, R. G.
Hastings, George
Hale, J. L.
Haslett, Dr. John
Hodgkins, Thomas
Hatheway, Mrs. H. C.
Hance, W. C.
Hayes, J. J.
Hatfield, Wm.
Hampson, R. J.
Harman, Mrs.
Hathway, Miss S.
Isaacs, John S.
Johnson, S. E.
Johnson, Mrs. J.
Jenks, Henry
Johnson, J. J.
Johnson, Jeremiah
King, John B.
Kellogg, Mrs.
King, Gamaliel
Low, A. A.
Lee, Wm.
Lott, John F.
Leavitt, Edward
Lyon, Robert A.
Lyon, George
Lewis, Rev. W. H.
Lefferts, R.
Lee, ——
Leverich, D. T.
Milne, Peter
Moody, Henry
Morse, Dr. John F.
Madden, Louisa S.
Messenger, Thomas
Mason, Nehemiah
Morrison, Miss Anna
Merrifield, Mrs.
Marvin, Dr. George
Messenger, H.
Morgan, Mrs. S.
Miller, J. E.
Masterton, W. J.
Marston, Wm.
Munn, Wm.
Morris, Miss
McGowan, Mrs. E.
McGeorge, Thomas
McDonald, W.
McBurney, Thomas, Jr.
McClellan, Dr. C. R.
McKee, J. W.
Naylor, John
Nichols, M. C. E.
Nufeldt, Louisa
Osborn, A. H.
Ostrander, Dr. ——
Ostrom, A. P.
O'Hara, Peter
Olmstead, W. B.
Owen, Mrs.
Osborn, J. W.
Perry, J. A.
Pierrepont, H. E.
Peck, Wm. M.
Patchen, Henry
Patrick, Mrs. A
Parker, Wm.
Pitbladdo, W.
Pearsall, J.
Powell, Henry
Pearsall, S.
Parmlee, Mrs. A. O.
Pierrepont, Mrs. H. B.
Roberts, J.

Ritter, Mrs. M.
Ryders, Clarkson W.
Ritter, Mrs. Eleanor
Rosman, Dr. R.
Robertson, Wm.
Rorker, Mrs. C. A.
Russell, Henry
Rogers, Mrs. A.
Richards, Mrs. A.
Richards, B.
Rogers, T.
Redding, Thomas H.
Ransom, B.
Stryker, Francis B.
Stilwell, G. W.
Sidell, A. H.
Stilwell, B. M.
Storry, Rowland
Sprague, Wm. E.
Sneckner, Wm.
Stryker, B.
Storry, Robert R.
Stephenson, Frederick
Schoonmaker, Mrs.
Sherman, J. W.
Sawyer, Miss H. A.
Smith, J. A.
Spooner, A. J.
Smith, J. C.
Spinola, F.
Sheldon, Leavitt
Smith, Lucius
Smith, C. P.
Swift, Samuel
Spies, F. A.
Stone, Rev. Dr.
Stebbins, Asa
Scrimgeour, Wm.
Spear, Calvin
Seaman, D. K.
Spooner, Henry
Swertcope, John
Shipley, Thomas
Shepard, J. H.
Tomsey, A.
Tempest, Thomas
Titus, C. H.
Tombs, A.
Thompson, S.
Taylor, E. E. L.
Thompson, S. W.
Talmadge, Thomas G.
Terry, Henry
Underhill, J.
Utter, Samuel S.
Underhill, Alexander
Underhill, Clarkson
Volmer, John A.
Van Dyke, John
Van Ness, Dr. J.
Van Brunt, N.
Voorhees, Judah B.
Van Voorhees, Miss A. S.
Van Nostrand, A.
Voorhies, J.
Van Brunt, W. B.
Van Brunt, Adriance
Van Brunt, John A.
Van Benschoten, Samuel
Wadsworth, G. B.
Weeks, Willet
White, Miss Martha
White, Edward D
White, S., Jr.
Wilkinson, M.
Wheelwright, G.
Whitlock, E. J.
White, T.
Wadsworth, Washington
Wood, C.

NAMES OF THE ORIGINAL SUBSCRIBERS.

Wilkins, Mrs. Henry
White, Mrs. H. C.
Whitman, Alexander A.
Weed, Mrs. M.
Wyckoff, H. S.
Wells, Dr. P. P.
Wyckoff, Van Brunt
Westervelt, Mrs. J.
Wilson, Joseph
Wood, J. G.
Wilhelmina & Brunson
Wood, John Jay
Whittelsey, Elisha
Webster, Hosea

BOSTON, MASS.

Abbott, Dr. S. L., Jr.
Alexander, Charles A.
Adams, Dr. Z. B.
Atkins, Issiah
Appleton, S.
Appleton, N.
Appleton, Mrs. T. A.
Adams, Benjamin
Allen, Freeman
Adams, C. F.
Bowditch, J. Ingersoll
Brimmer, Martin
Boles, John
Boynton, G. W.
Bush, James P.
Bradlee, Josiah
Brigham, Levi
Burton, Hazen J.
Blackburn, George
Bayley, Samuel K.
Blanchard, Wm. B.
Brown, Jonathan
Blanchard, Wm. G.
Bacon, Daniel C.
Blanchard, John A.
Brooks, Edward
Burgess, B. F.
Bond, George Wm.
Barnes, D. W.
Brewster, J.
Converse, James C.
Colley, Benjamin E.
Carey, Alpheus
Codman, Edward
Curtis, Nathan
Cushing, Thomas P.
Cary, Isaac H.
Cochrane, S. Q.
Cooke, Josiah P.
Curtis, Samuel S.
Curtis, J. F.
Cooper, Robert
Cotting, Amos
Carter, R. B.
Darracott, George
Dana, A. N.
Davis, Thomas
Dexter, Thomas A.
Dodd, James
Dana, Samuel
Davis, Henry
Dewhurst, Wm.
Doane, Miss C.
Dixwell, J. J.
Davis, J., Jr.
Eliot, Samuel A.
Edwards, J. W.

Eldridge, O.
Fales, Mrs. Samuel
Flint, Waldo
Francis, Nathan
Fairbanks, H. P.
Farnham, Henry
Frothingham, Samuel
Forbes, F. H.
Fairfield, John
Foster, Joseph
Fletcher, Richard
Fuller, Henry H.
Goodwin, Ozias
Goodrich, Ira
Gould, James
Greenough, Wm.
Goodrich, C. B.
Gregg, Dr. Samuel
Gould, B. A.
Gray, J. C.
Glover, Henry R.
Greene, D.
Heard, Augustine
Hosmer, Zelotes
Huntington, L. A.
Hedge, Frank
Hunt, N.
Hanscombe, A.
Howe, Joseph N., Jr
Harvey, Peter
Howe, George
Hewins, Samuel K.
Hennessey, Edward
Heard, Mrs. John
Hooper, Robert
Howe, I. L.
Henderson, Charles
Hall, A. T.
Inches, Miss
Jones, Eliphalet
Jameson, Wm. H.
Johnson, James B.
Jones, Cyrus
Kimball, Daniel
Kelleher, John
Karuth, Nathan
Kendall, Abel
Kuhn, G. H.
Lawrence, Abbott
Lee, Sarah
Loring, John G.
Lloyd, Daniel
Lamson, J.
Loring, Henry
Lobdell, T. J.
Loring, Benjamin
Lewis, S. S.
Lovejoy, W. B.
Locke, Lyman
Leland, Sherman
Lothrop, S. K.
Locke, Charles A.
Lawrence, Amos A.
Lincoln, M. S.
Lawrence, Wm.
Lewis, Joseph
Low, Dr. A. S.
Mayo, Edward R.
Messenger, G. W.
May, John
Mead, Samuel O.
Miles, Walter
Mills, Charles
McBurney, C.
Norcross, Otis
Nolen, S., Jr.
Newhall, D. B.

Noble, Wm.
Oliver, Francis J.
Oxnard, H. P.
Pope, Lemuel
Perkins, Mary T.
Parker, Charles H.
Parker, John W.
Pope, H. K.
Putnam, Catharine
Parker, Isaac
Parker, W. H.
Parker, Peter
Perry, Thomas
Parker, Daniel P.
Prince, John T.
Richards, Reuben
Rogers, George
Robbins, E. H.
Reynolds, Edwin
Read & Chadwick
Russell, James
Rich, Benjamin
Rand, L.
Robinson, J. P.
Read, Wm.
Rice, Israel C.
Raymond, Edward A.
Rollins, Mrs. E.
Reed, G. P.
Reynolds, Wm.
Sturgis, Russell
Shattuck, Dr. George C.
Stearns, Joseph G.
Snow, H. A.
Skinner, S. N.
Smith & Sumner
Sewall, S. E.
Stedman, D. B.
Shaw, Charles B.
Stone, Wm. W.
Snow, Mrs. Thomas
Stone, Henry B.
Swett, S.
Savage, James
Shaw, Robert G.
Smart, Mrs. Ann
Sargent, L. M.
Sumner, S. A.
Simpson, M. H.
Sibley, Henry
Tudor, Frederick
Tirrell, Edward C.
Tappan, John
Tisdale, M.
Taylor, Richard
Thompson, N. A.
Tucker, John L.
Throw, Samuel T.
Trull, John
Tremlet, Mrs. F.
Trull, John W.
Thwing, S. C.
Thayer, B. W.
Varney, Mrs. George R.
Wigglesworth, Mrs. T.
Williams, Henry L.
Whiting, Caleb
Wilder, Marshall P.
Willis, Nathaniel
Witherbee, J. B
Williams, David W.
Weld, John D.
Whall, Joseph B.
Winslow, George
Warren, S. D.
Walley, Samuel H., Jr.
Wetherell, John

Whiton, J. P.
Winsor, N., Jr.
Welles, Mrs.
Wolcott, J. H.
Watts, Miss
Webb, G. J.
Whittemore, Augustus
Winter, F. B.

PROVIDENCE, R. I.

Allen, Zachariah
Dennis, D. L.
Foster, F. F.
Kent, Dr. J. Emerson
King, Wm. J.
Kelly, Alexander
Knight, J. C.
Lockwood, M. B.
Mathewson, Miss P.
Paine, Mrs. Amarancy
Sawin, E. D.
Smith, Richard
Taylor, Richard R.
Warren, Russell
White, Thomas
Wilson, Samuel S.

FLATBUSH, L. I.

Bogardus, C. S.
Bogardus, Mrs. Gilbert M.
Crook, Mrs. Philip S.
Duryee, Miss Helen N.
Duryee, Mrs. C.
Green, Wm. H.
Johnson, David
Lott, Mrs. Ann M.
Lott, Mrs. Mary
Martense, Mrs. Helen
Murphy, Thomas
Robinson, Dr. ——
Robinson, D.
Stilenworth, Jacob
Storer, Edward
Vanderhilt, John
Varina, Charles
Vanderbilt, John, Jr.
Willink, J. A.

Williamsburgh, L. I.

Barrow, Lawrence
Bartlett, Mrs. ——
Duncan, F.
McNeil, J.
Sammis, Edson A.
Wakeman, Walter
Young, Mrs. J. S.

JAMAICA, L. I.

Hagner, Henry J.
Hogan, Mrs. Michael
Kelsey, Thomas H.
Mills, N. S.
Nelson, Benjamin S.

Smith, Anthony M
Spader, John

NEW UTRECHT, L. I.

Bennett, Winant
Denier, Jacob

Flushing, L. I.

Peck, Mrs. ——

DETROIT, MICH.

Ledyard, Henry

STOCKBRIDGE, MASS.

Dresser, J. B.

TORONTO, CANADA.

Harris, T. D.

MIDDLETOWN, CONN.

Duffield, Mrs.

HARTFORD, CONN.

Batterson, James G

Jersey City, N. J.

Chadeayne, Mary J.
Gregory, J. G.
Gregory, D. S.
Henderson, D.
James, J. B.
Jordan, Mrs.
McClelland, R. B.
Rathbun, H.

NEWARK, N. J.

Alling, Horace
Crocket, Mrs.
Duncombe, C. T.
Grant, Charles
Johnson, Mrs.

PATERSON, N. J.

Van Houten, Mrs.

☞ *Subscribers' names omitted in this list will be given at the conclusion of the Mount-Auburn series.*

CPSIA information can be obtained
at www.ICGtesting.com
Printed in the USA
BVHW011147120921
616617BV00016B/979